Leaving Prison
FOR GOOD

Everything the Ex-Inmate Needs to Know and Do to Re-enter Society Self-Rehabilitated and Recidivism-Proof

by LONZY F. EDWARDS

Magnolia Publishing Company
Macon, Georgia

Notice:
The information in this book does not give general solutions that can be applied to every apparently similar problem faced by an inmate or former inmate. Since changes in the facts of a case may require different advice, the contents of this book should not be used to solve legal problems.

Printed in the United States of America

ISBN No.: 0-9657451-4-7

Library of Congress Catalog Card Number: 2009931228

DEDICATION

To the long-suffering children, spouses, parents, grandparents, and friends of prisoners who will re-enter society and their lives in the hope that when they come home it will be for good.

TABLE OF CONTENTS

PREFACE

This book is the product of a series of life experiences, reflections on things I have read, and observations over the last thirty years. I have seen many people in your predicament in my capacity as a lawyer and minister. However, what I have to say is not based on having spent time in jail or prison. Rather, it is based on what I have learned about how to succeed in spite of having grown up in a single parent family on welfare without spending a day behind bars. You already know about jail or prison. There is little that I or anyone else can teach you about it. Now success – that is a different matter. What I offer in this book is coaching on how to succeed in life outside of prison in the real world where the game of life is played instead of sitting on the bench in a penalty box or some other place where those who are disqualified to play are sent.

There are lots of ways to succeed. Some of them work better than others. There are undoubtedly people who have helped people like you make it with advice that is quite different from what I offer. But by having picked up this book, you have allowed me to be your mentor, and in the pages that follow I will tell you how I suggest that you do it.

Despite the fact that in the words of Langston Hughes, "life for me ain't been no crystal stair," I have had a great life. Only in America can a poor boy get out of abject poverty through honest means by going to school and trying to "make something out of himself."

By the grace of God, I earned four degrees. I have worked as a teacher and a minister-lawyer. I have also worked in local government as an appointed and elected official. Based on this preparation and life experience, I believe I am qualified to offer a word of counsel to you.

There is always the assumption in some circles that if you have not experienced the same problem that the people you are trying to help are dealing with that it somehow invalidates what you have to say. As one does not have to put his hand in fire to know it will burn, a person who is in touch with his or her humanity can empathize with and help people who are suffering from something he or she has not experienced. Many of the world's best oncologists have never had cancer. That is true of lawyers who have never been convicted of anything, psychiatrists who have not been psychotic, cardiologists who have never had a heart attack, counselors who have never been alcoholics or addicts, and many other medical and social science practitioners who are working to find solutions to problems that they do not have. Some of the best coaches in professional and college sports were not good enough to play at the level where they are now coaching.

In evaluating what I say, take what you can use and discard the rest. The mark of a wise person is willingness to take light from whatever source he or she can find it. I trust that the insights I share will be experienced as light on the dark path you are now traveling.

I appreciatively acknowledge that writing this book would not have been possible without the help and encouragement of a lot of good people. Sitting in the course entitled, "Developing An Effective Prison Ministry" in the Congress of Christian Education of the National Baptist Convention, USA, Inc, taught by Rev. D. Grady Scott with the assistance of Lee Boone in 2008, gave me a fresh perspective on the importance of this work and convinced me of the merit of this project. In addition to thanking them, I gratefully acknowledge the influence of the teaching and writing of Dr. Anthony Kelly on my thinking. I am indebted to Teresa Johnson, Belinda Wilmore, and Dot Appling for faithfully laboring to prepare the manuscript. I also acknowledge my indebtedness to Dr. Jim Marshall, Dr. Catherine Meeks, Dr. Anna Holloway and Ms. Joni Woolf for taking the time to offer editorial assistance and many constructive suggestions which greatly improved this book. I am solely responsible for any errors or omissions in this work. I commend it to you in humble recognition that as there are no perfect people, it follows that there are no perfect books – or anything else!

PART I

INTRODUCTION
What This Book Is About

To begin with, what I say is primarily addressed to you, regardless of whether you are still behind bars, about to be released, or already outside of jail or prison. There are those who ask, "Why bother?" They ask this question because they mistakenly believe that you do not read books. That might be true of books that talk down to you. It may also be true of books that are irrelevant to people in your predicament. I would not read such books and would not blame you for not reading them. In this book I say something that speaks directly to you in a firm, but respectful way. Instead of getting in your face, I try to get into your head. Of necessity, it is gently confrontational in tone. I invite you to push back against what I say because I am convinced that Ralph Waldo Emerson was right when he said, "No man thoroughly understands a truth until he has contended against it."[1]

We are being shaped and sharpened even when we do not realize it. That is one of the unappreciated and sometimes unintended consequences of adversity and a relationship with a person who is hard on us. Butting heads with someone whose head is at least as hard as yours makes both of you better. This is one of the main reasons one should be extremely careful about his or her associates. A lot of us are bent out of shape. The people you hang around have great potential to shape your thinking and behavior. Hopefully, that is what will happen as a result of reading this book, because as King Solomon observed centuries ago, "As iron sharpens iron, so one man sharpens another" (Proverbs 27:17 NIV).

I was asked, why write a book on this subject? Some good people say, "With all the things that have been written, those people have not changed. Will you say anything different?" I am not sure I would read anything that is demeaning or dehumanizing. I try very hard to avoid these faults and to be respectful of my primary audience—you. That is why I try to speak directly to you, not about you. Most books about people in your circumstances are written for someone else because of the belief that you do not buy or read books. What I have to say is different not only in the advice it offers, but also in its effort to speak directly to you and not about you. I think the perception of you is wrong. I believe you will accept constructive criticism and godly counsel. It is for this reason that I have cast my "bread upon the waters."

While going to jail or prison is the last thing any right-thinking person would ever consciously do, it is not the end of the world, and what matters is what you learned from your experience and what you do with the rest of your life. As wise people have observed for a long time, "Where you are going is more important than where you have been." This book offers constructive advice to help you get a good, fresh start-over on the first days of the rest of your life.

It is hard for people to hear the truth under the best of circumstances. But it is even more difficult when the truth is not spoken with love. As the object of any book is communication, I want you to at least hear what I say even if you do not agree with it. That is why the truth I present is shared with love. Besides, only "the truth will set you free." I realize that sometimes the truth hurts. But that is a small price to pay for the healing and freedom that come when it is courageously faced and accepted.

Many of you started your criminal careers at a young age. What was laughed at and considered cute eventually became criminal. For too many of you, getting in trouble was a "rite of passage." The juvenile justice system was your first contact with a regimented environment. From there you graduated to the local jail, which was just another step along the way in your progression from petty crime to the kind of behavior that got you put in prison.

Prison for most of you is a "lifetime achievement award." That means that you have had one chance after another and did nothing with it. You wouldn't go to school, and if you went, you goofed off. Eventually you probably stopped or got kicked out. You got probation, but went back to prison because you wouldn't change. You got parole and still would not do right. It may be that prison was society's last resort in dealing with you.

Although I am sure you know it, there are people who do not realize that a jail is a short-term local detention facility. Large numbers of people in jail are awaiting trial or some other disposition of the charges against them. A prison, unlike a jail, is for the long term incarceration of people who are convicted. According to Angela Y. Davis, "Most people are unaware of the fact that jail and prison are two different institutions."[2] She says, "More than half of the jail population has never been convicted of anything." Somebody forgot to tell lexicographers who use the words jail and prison interchangeably about this distinction. For want of a better, inclusive, term I use the word prison to describe both places of lawful confinement, except when a specific context requires the use of either jail or prison. Regardless of whether it is the population of jails or prisons, the number of people who are in there is not only shocking, but also sobering. A disproportionate number of those who are in jails and prisons are African-Americans. By some estimates as many as 700,000 people leave state and federal prisons each year. But the annual population of local jails is a staggering nine million. In some instances, the population of local jails is 80 percent or more African American.[3] All of us have probably heard the claim that "there are more young African-American men behind bars than in college." This or a similar statement has been made by Sen. Barrack Obama[4] during his successful run for the presidency and many other politicians.

While it is fashionable for social critics and politicians to make this statement, it is not completely accurate. The reality is that there are "twice as many black men 18-24 in college as there are in jail.[5]" The late Johnnie J. Cochran said, "It frightens me that our young black men have a better chance of going to jail than going to college."[6] This is closer to the truth. What is said of African-American young men is becoming true of Hispanics and other non-white people in America. Why this is happening is almost always attributed to racism. But one should beware of simplistic, single explanations of something this complex, especially when someone's goal is to shift responsibility for his or her circumstances to someone else. Another factor to be considered is the increasingly large number of white people and women of all races who have gotten caught up in the prison system. This suggests that what is often attributed to race may be better explained on the basis of class and character. In any event, the explanation of this phenomenon is beyond the scope of this book. Its more modest task is to help those who are leaving the system keep from reentering it—and those who are entering it prepare for the day when they will regain their freedom, regardless of their race. The cost to a community is just as great when young men and women throw their lives away, regardless of whether they are black, white, Hispanic or a member of some other non-white racial group. After all, people are people, and those who end up behind bars are no less deserving of help than anyone else just because they happen to be of a particular race.

In addressing this subject, I attempt to consistently use gender-inclusive language. Although the percentage of women in prison is growing, the overwhelming majority of inmates are male. What I say is equally applicable to men and women.

I also attempt to use race-neutral language whenever possible although in many local jails the population is overwhelming African American. The term African American and black are used interchangeably.

I approach this task from an interdisciplinary perspective as a minister and lawyer with over thirty years of experience. As a minister, I have seen the wrecked lives of individuals that were caused by drugs, alcohol, poverty, fatherlessness, irresponsible decision-making and mal-parenting. Functioning as a lawyer gave me another opportunity to observe what happens when people would not hear parents, ministers, police officers, teachers, and coaches and are forced to listen to judges, guards and wardens. Although I am proud of the time I spent in the legal profession, the perspective from which I approach this subject is pastoral care. Pastoral care involves the process of shepherding people through the crises and ordinary circumstances of life through counseling, teaching, and preaching for those who can be reached in a church setting. For those who are hurting and feel alienated from God, family members, the Church, and themselves, this book may be not just the next best thing, but also the only thing to reach you where you are. For this reason, I do not apologize for confronting you with truth that makes you uncomfortable. That is the motive and effect of preaching that leads to change. According to pastoral care theorists, there are at least four ways to conceive this work:

Guiding, which is another way of talking about counseling, designed to help troubled people make decisions; Healing, which is the process through which individuals, families, relationships and institutions achieve wholeness, and rise above their circumstances; Sustaining, which refers to the role of care givers in helping hurting people get through or cope with circumstances from which there may not be a means of escape; and Reconciling, which attempts to achieve a renewal of relationships between people who are estranged from each other and God.[7]

These functions are relevant to a person who is in a crisis, regardless of where he or she is in serving a sentence. Consequently, there is something in this book which addresses the various stages of incarceration and release.

In a prison setting, the guards, counselors, warden, and other staff members may have issues involving their work with you that require the same kind of care you need. This is a result of the tremendous stress their jobs cause. Believe it or not, despite what you heard about sadistic guards at the infamous Abu Ghraib prison in Iraq, and possibly other prisons, most of them are good people who take no pleasure in seeing you locked-up, do not mistreat prisoners, and would like nothing better than to see you leave their custody for good. They represent what is good in our society and care about your welfare. The proof is their willingness to be locked up with you! For most, it is not just a job, but a way to fulfill their life's calling. Without them, your life would have been far worse—and you might not have survived your experience, physically, emotionally or psychologically. That is why they are deserving of honor and respect. Besides, they are the authorities that you are subject to behind bars. You might as well get used to having someone to answer to in jail or prison. It will help you do it like everyone else when you are released. Being in an environment where you are exposed to people whose values are anti-social and behavior is aberrant, it is easy to understand how a person in your position can lose track of what it means to be human, sane, or socially acceptable. Your most immediate model of humanity and sanity is the staff of the jail or prison. This is why interaction and cooperation with them to the extent allowed by prison security regulations is a good idea. Their compassion will help influence you to be a compassionate human being and give you a standard by which to test reality. If you follow this advice, do not be surprised if some of your fellow prisoners accuse you of "sucking up" or worse. I realize that this flies in the face of the tenet of the "convict code" which requires you to distrust prison officials who are col-lectively called "the man." Whether you agree with it or not, guards are there for your protection. They serve as agents of the state for the same purpose that is performed by policemen in our communities. (See Romans 13.)

Before you decide how to handle this issue, perhaps you should pause and remem-ber what caring too much about what folks think who do not have your best interest at heart has gotten you. How you are treated behind bars will influence how you treat people in and out of prison. That depends largely on you, your attitude, and conduct. Prison conditions are meant to be Spartan or difficult. But they do not have to be bar-baric. I agree with Fyodor Dostoevsky: "The degree of civilization in a society can be judged by entering its prisons."[8] Were it not for the good people who have dedicated their lives to helping people like you, the "degree of civilization" in our society would be small indeed, given the large number of people who are constantly re-entering our communities after spending time in prison. That is why what I have written in these pages is not just for you, but also law enforcement officials, chaplains, prison officials, parole officers, members of your family, and other good people who are trying to help you.

As a minister, I believe there is good in the worst of us. Yet, I am under no illusions about our potential for evil. As a lawyer, I have seen people at their worst, and I know we are capable of doing some ugly, bad things. Let's face it, many people are incorrigible. However, this book reflects my belief in the potential of most people for redemption. Its goal is to help people who are capable of redemption make the adjustments in their beliefs and thinking to reach their goal of becoming a decent, law abiding, contributing member of society.

There are some people who cannot survive outside of a regimented jail or prison environment. They, for whatever reason, are incapable of controlling their impulses, tempers and behavior. Consequently, they are always in trouble and in jail or prison. They just can not quit lying, stealing, conning, "hustling," or committing violent acts. For many of them, especially the violent offenders, there will always be a need for jails or prisons. This book may help even those who are in this category because one never knows when a person will see the light. I refuse to believe the conventional wisdom which says "once a con always a con."

On the other hand, there are people who are tired of a life of crime and isolation from the people they love. These are people who have decided that it is time to make a change and live life the way it is supposed to be lived because whatever crime paid them, when they considered what they lost, it just was not worth it. This may just be the time that an important lesson has been learned—when a light finally goes off in their heads. If you are in this category, this book is primarily for your benefit—and your family members and friends who are committed to salvaging you from the scrap heap of life. All adversity is not bad. Whether it is good or bad depends upon whether you learn anything from it that makes you a better person.

Whether you fall in the former or latter category is up to you. No one can consign you to the category of people who need to be locked up or the group that has seen the light but you. You can move from a state of hopelessness to one with reasonably good prospects any time you are ready. For your sake and that of your aging parents, spouses, children, and boyfriends or girlfriends, I hope it is sooner rather later. What I have written is offered in the hope that it will help you make good on a commitment to be a better person if that is what you have done. Until that happens, nothing anyone says to you will make any difference in how your life turns out.

Let me say a word about what this book is not. It is not a treatise on the law, which can be used to solve any of your legal problems. Consequently, it should not be used for this purpose. While there may be occasional references to legal issues, they are included only for the purpose of clarifying various aspects of an inmate's or ex-inmate's situation and promoting understanding of the hurdles that must be overcome. Regardless, what is presented here is not intended and should not be used as a substitute for the advice of your legal counsel. I believe that at this point in your life, you have a far greater need for non-legal advice than anything that may be obtained from a lawyer.

Many of you have had access to some pretty good lawyers your entire criminal career, and they did not do you any good with the issue that matters the most—rehabilitation and character repair. Perhaps it is time to listen to another perspective.

Because you have a higher purpose than just doing time behind bars, recidivism is not an option for any but the most hopeless, hapless, and hardened among you. Hopefully, you are not in either category. The underlying assumptions of this book are as follows:

1. When you get lost, it is possible to get back on the right track through spiritual and pastoral redirection;
2. Character flaws can be corrected, and no one is beyond redemption;
3. Incarceration is not something to be proud of or forever do penance for;
4. Mistakes in how one lives his or her life do not necessarily make him or her a bad person;
5. Rehabilitation is a matter of personal and social responsibility, but the primary responsibility belongs to the individual;
6. Recidivism is not inevitable because of the possibility of change in the way people think and behave; and
7. Having a jail or prison record does not deprive a person of his or her humanity.

Understanding What You Are Up Against

In trying to solve every social problem by locking people up, taxpayers have become, for all intents and purposes, prisoners of the individuals we lock up. It has been observed that when doctors make mistakes, they are handled by undertakers who bury them and when lawyers make mistakes they are written up in law books for other lawyers to study. When we fail as a society, we either execute the persons with whom we failed or lock them up as long as possible. For many citizens, the attitude is "out of sight and out of mind." It is a way of denying society's responsibility for failing schools and deteriorating families. Systems theory holds that there is enough fault to go around. What that means is that because of the influence of the parts of society on the whole, what happens in one part of our system can not help but affect the others.

The sooner we figure out that we can't lock everybody up who makes a mistake, the better off our society will be. We can't afford to build enough jails, hire enough police officers, and create enough courts to lock up everybody. In some communities, more money is spent on jail and prison cells than on classrooms, and we know that it costs less to educate a person than to incarcerate him or her. The numbers are shocking: $25,000.00 per year to incarcerate a person and depending on the affluence of the community,[9] approximately $6,000.00 to educate a person. For my money, there is too little emphasis on crime prevention. But as long as criminals terrorize their community, elected officials will spare no expense to deal with crime, no matter how many tax dollars are required. That is true even though virtually everybody who goes to jail or prison eventually ends up back on our streets—and ultimately in our communities as our neighbors, co-workers, and fellow citizens. Whether you find acceptance or rejection depends more on you than the people whom you will encounter. If you resort to what got you into trouble, people will treat you the same way you were treated before. But if you show that you have changed, people will respond to you in a different way.

Getting to the point of accepting your present circumstances is likely to be a tortuous process. We grieve all kinds of losses, not just death or divorce. The loss that you will grieve is loss of your freedom and separation from your family members and friends regardless of whether you are in prison for the first time or been in "the joint" several times. What was talked about by older writers like Elizabeth Kubler-Ross in connection with death and dying is equally applicable to other losses in life. The typical stages of grief are denial, bargaining, anger, depression, and acceptance. No one goes through them in the same order.[10] The important thing is to work your way through them and hopefully end up at acceptance. That is the point at which a person finds peace—and can move forward with the rest of his or her life. Too many get stuck in denial, anger, or depression, with disastrous results. These are probably the people who are in and out of trouble all the time, or who are psychologically destroyed by their time in prison.

At some point, each prisoner or former prisoner has to realize that the time for technical objections and appeals is over, regardless of the illegality of the initial arrest, denials of basic constitutional rights, allegations of systemic racism, the incompetence of legal counsel, or bias of the judge and jury, in order to move on. When that happens is for you to decide. We know that the system is not perfect and occasionally results in wrongful convictions. Witnesses have been known to lie and some prosecutors and policemen have been shown to have distorted or destroyed evidence. In some communities, racial profiling still occurs. Given the frequency of this kind of activity by "rogue" public officials, no one should blame you for continuing to deny your guilt and pursuing your dream of vindication, in spite of your conviction. But that is a double-edged sword. It may have gotten you a longer sentence because protesting your innocence was interpreted as a lack of remorse or refusal to accept responsibility by the trial judge. It may also come back to haunt you when you apply for parole if it is seen as proof that you are not rehabilitated. That is why you must be honest with yourself about your guilt. Let's get real! Everybody in prison is not there because of a wrongful conviction. When I practiced criminal law, I rarely had a "guilty" client, until the trial date arrived and my client saw the make-up of the jury and decided that a plea bargain was in his best interest after all. As shocking as it is, the law sometimes values finality more highly than getting every case right—despite pious claims that it is better that "the guilty go free than for an innocent person to be imprisoned." There are those who will excuse themselves for thinking this with the observation that you might not be guilty this time of the offense which you are now in prison for, but there is no need to get "heartburn" about it because you were probably guilty on other occasions and got off or did not get caught. For them your incarceration means that the system is catching up and getting even—like the stock market. They believe that when a jury returns a verdict of not guilty, it does not necessarily mean that no crime was committed. It could mean it was not proved "beyond a reasonable doubt." Fortunately, through DNA evidence many wrongfully convicted prisoners have been vindicated. Too often they are set free with little or no compensation for the injustice that was perpetrated against them.

It is increasingly clear that DNA evidence is having a profound effect on the way guilt and innocence are determined and attitudes about fair compensation for wrongful convictions. This evidence has resulted in the release of more than two hundred people since 1989. Of that number, 38 percent have not received any compensation for the time they were wrongly incarcerated.

Of the more than 140 exonerated prisoners released since 2000, twenty-two states and the District of Columbia have started to compensate them through lump payments as calculation of lost wages. But there is no uniformity in how compensation is provided. For example, Wisconsin provides $5,000 a year for a maximum of five years. California pays $100 a day, and Tennessee pays up to a $1 million total. Twenty-eight states do not pay anything, and that forces wrongfully convicted people to sue in state or federal court, where in order to prevail, they must bear the burden of showing that their conviction resulted from bad faith or intended misconduct by officials. Curiously, one of the arguments of opponents of compensation for exonerated prisoners is that those with a "history of serious crimes" should not be compensated. It is as if they are saying if they had not been a bad person on previous occasions they wouldn't be in the mess they are in now!

Money is only part of the problem of making a wrongfully convicted person whole. People in this category are not likely to have the means to reintegrate themselves into society. Only Massachusetts, Louisiana, and Vermont pay the costs of medical and psychological care.[11]

If you had the misfortune to commit a capital offense in Texas, you have a significantly greater likelihood of receiving a death sentence. In fact, more than 60 percent of all American executions took place in Texas at a time when several states were imposing moratoriums on the death penalty. The result is that there are fewer executions, which was related by one critic to the possibility of exoneration if a wrongfully convicted person is put to death.[12]

I want to help you discover the person you were meant to be through a process of regeneration, renewal, or personal transformation. The process of being reborn is never static. We are always in the process of becoming. That is true of everything worthwhile because "life is a process or journey rather than a destination or event." Consequently, one never arrives. Since most of us develop only a small part of our potential, there is always something for us to work on.

You can choose the person you want to be. This book is offered to help you in this process. In addition, it offers help in overcoming the stigma of criminality, staying out of trouble, and re-entering society. What you do with it and the rest of your life is up to you.

This book was designed to be used in conjunction with formal cognitive skills sessions, cognitive behavioral therapy, and re-entry programs. It was also designed to be used by an individual who wants to begin the process of rehabilitation on his or her own. It is divided into three parts. In Part Two, I describe the challenge you face and try to make the case for each person to assume responsibility for his or her rehabilitation. Part Three consists of the issues and adjustments in your beliefs and thoughts that are necessary to maximize your chance of succeeding outside of jail or prison. It also presents practical advice on how to deal with the various aspects of rejoining society after incarceration. While you can begin by reading either section first, I suggest that if you are still incarcerated and read only one part, it should be section two, in order to begin the mental and spiritual preparation for release long before it happens. This section, I submit, will not only help you make the requisite pre-release changes in thinking and beliefs, but also provide invaluable assistance in readjusting to society. Some of what I say is equally applicable to the pre-release and post-release phase of your life—and there is some overlap or repetition in the subsections that will help inculcate the points that are made.

Let me be the first to wish you well on your journey towards wholeness and responsible membership in society. The road will not be easy. Too many turn back! It is, as Robert Frost put it, "a road less traveled." But if you stay on it, you can salvage the rest of your life. My prayer is that your testimony "somewhere ages and ages hence" will reflect the experience of Frost: "Two roads diverged in the woods, and I—I took the one less traveled by, and that has made all the difference."[13]

PART II

PRE-RELEASE LIFE PREPARATION:
What You Need To Know and Do

Although William James said it first, Napoleon Hill is usually credited with the observation that "whatever the mind of man can conceive and believe it can achieve." Regardless of who said it, the point is that if you cannot see yourself doing something even before you attempt it, your chances of being successful in doing it are remote. That is why a necessary component of your preparation for release from jail or prison is changing the way you think and what you believe. You cannot wait until you are out of jail or prison to begin this process. It should begin as soon as possible. In my experience, it is impossible to correct behavior without confronting and straightening out "stinking thinking"—and flawed beliefs. As behavior follows what is thought and believed at the deepest level of your being, that is the point of departure for our journey together in this section.

CHAPTER ONE
Accepting Responsibility
for Your Rehabilitation

There are theorists who believe that rehabilitation should not be used as the main objective of sentencing—and corrections. Instead, in this view, the function of the correctional system should be to isolate and punish criminals in order to protect society because that is all it knows how to do.[1] This point of view is increasingly accepted by average citizens as shown by a 1970 Harris poll which found that 73 percent of Americans "thought that the primary purpose of prison should be rehabilitation," but by 1995 only 26 percent did."[2] I submit that for many it is not just a matter of not knowing what to do. We know that education and vocational training work. But for most people, I suspect they just do not believe that criminals can be changed or that they can change themselves. I would like nothing better than to help you prove them wrong about you. We know that a majority of ex-prisoners are "male, minority, and unskilled" and that they have been "incarcerated many times, have a long history of alcoholism, and drug use, have probably been involved in gangs and drug selling, been unemployed, had periods of homelessness, and some have physical and mental health issues."[3] In fact, the overwhelming majority of people behind bars are male. According to the National Urban League, "Per 100,000 people, black men have an incarceration rate that is over 20 times that of black women."[4]

Several prison systems handle the increase in inmates by using facilities that were never intended to serve this purpose such as tents on prison grounds, gymnasiums, day rooms, educational meeting rooms, and treatment rooms. In addition, private prisons often used to deal with overcrowding and local jails were contracted with governmental agencies to hold 77,987 more state and federal inmates in 2006.

Two-thirds of ex-inmates will be arrested; almost one-half of this population will be sent back to prison for a new offence or technical violation of the terms of their release; and almost one-fourth will be sent back to prison for a new conviction within three years of their release.[5]

That is why some prison officials tell departing inmates, "We'll see you" or "We'll leave the light on for you." Why give them the satisfaction of saying, "I told you so" when you show back up as they predicted? While some of you will stay on the right course from the day of your release, for others, what will happen will not be clear for at least three years. For you, "the jury will be out" for a long time before it is apparent that you have been reformed or learned your lesson. The test is not what you say when you leave prison. Rather, it is what you are doing three years later. Whatever mental and spiritual condition that caused you to be an offender has to remain in remission for about this long for your rehabilitation to be considered a success. Too many people quit and end up back in prison.

There is little doubt that there is a connection between this bleak picture and the fact that "rehabilitation was replaced as the core mission of corrections with programs to deter and incapacitate."[6] Your prospects are made worse by laws which restrict access of people with a criminal record to public assistance, driver's licenses, food stamps, federally assisted housing, and public employment, and character requirements in such fields as medicine, law, dentistry, nursing, education, cosmetology, childcare, and home healthcare.[7]

If these impediments are not enough, even when there is no legal prohibition against employing a person with a record, an ex-prisoner's chances of obtaining work are reduced by the discrimination of employers who are legally permitted to consider convictions in making employment decisions.[8] There is a possibility that this conduct can violate federal anti-discrimination laws when there is a disparate impact on non-white applicants. But that is a long shot because there are few lawyers who are willing to take these cases, and your chances of winning them are so remote.

Regardless of your race, you will continue to face employment discrimination. If you are successful in getting a job, you may languish in the same position because of doubt about your ability to be trusted with "a responsible position" and you will be paid less than other employees.[9]

We know that legal employment is a primary indication of reintegration into "conventional society."[10] Yet we allow obstacles and impediments to something as basic as getting a job.[10]

Unfortunately, there are downturns in the economy that keep even well-qualified people who do not have a record from getting jobs. Under these circumstances, if you have a record, your changes of landing a good job are slim to none. That means you will either have to taka a job you would have never considered before or start a legitimate small business of your own.

The same can be said of marriage, which the law calls a fundamental right. We know that marriage, like legal employment, can connect a person to "conventional society."[11] A good or stable marriage gives an ex-inmate "emotional support upon release, an immediate place to live, and motivation to succeed." The people who have family ties while they are in prison "have high rates of post release success." The same is true of those who assume roles as husbands and parents.[12] This calls into question the less committed male-female relationships that so many are prone to live in, especially those who run from responsibility.

As important as marriage and family are, the law is not always "family friendly." The stress of incarceration is probably enough to cause the fragile ties that bind families to sever during incarceration. To make their situation worse, the law in some states may allow imprisonment to serve as grounds for termination of parental rights and divorce.[13]

If you don't clean up your act, you will cause your family to lose its housing if they are residing in public housing or housing obtained with a Section 8 voucher, because federal law requires that housing be denied to any household with a family member who is subject to a life-time obligation to comply with a registration requirement under a state sex offender program. Further, if you continue to use drugs or abuse alcohol there is a mandatory eviction requirement. Regardless of how much you are loved, it is too much to expect your family to sacrifice its housing to help you by allowing you to stay in violation of federal policies that can get them evicted.

An honest job is still the best deterrent to criminal behavior. It has been known for a long time that people who are unemployed are more likely to get into trouble. Yet not only do some employers refuse to hire them, there are other formidable obstacles to gainful employment[14] such as illegal discrimination.

But for all of the discrimination against ex-inmates, that is not the main obstacle to your ability to find employment. The biggest problem is your "behavior patterns that make holding a job difficult" as a result of being "embedded in criminality." Your bonds to "conventional society," including ties to families, jobs, and schools are weakened. When a person has lived a "criminal lifestyle," getting reconnected with "conventional society" is not easy—and this is one of the main reasons ex-inmates do not succeed in job training programs. Until you become motivated to work, job skills programs will not make any difference in your job prospects. Most scholars agree that a job and a skilled trade are not enough to solve an ex-inmate's problems.[15] Only when you deal with the underlying issues that are responsible for your criminal conduct can you expect to make it in the real world. No one can do this for you.

Black's Law Dictionary defines rehabilitation as "the process of seeking to improve a criminal's character and outlook so that he or she can function in society without committing other crimes."[16] The proof that no one can rehabilitate another person without his cooperation is the soaring rates of recidivism, which by definition is "a tendency to relapse into a habit of criminal behavior."[17] Usually, the recidivist has been found guilty of numerous crimes that are similar or the same. They are called "habitual offenders, habitual criminals, repeaters, and career criminals."

Rehabilitation, along with deterrence and retribution are theories of punishment that have been historically used by judges in dealing with convicted criminals and rationalizing the disposition of their cases. Measuring success in dealing with crime is virtually impossible on the basis of rehabilitation because it depends so much on the attitude and cooperation of the criminal. It can take years before any investment in rehabilitation programs produce results. But the other two depend solely on the judge, the Department of Corrections, and other parts of the criminal justice system. Locking people up and its effect on crime rates can be measured. If the relatively small number of "habitual criminals" are off the streets, they cannot commit crimes and the crime rate goes down. If they are executed, the argument goes, regardless of the effect on society, the deterrent effect is beyond dispute—at least with respect to the person who was put to death. Something similar happens when retribution is the goal. The state can do to a criminal what he or she did to his or her victim or something similar that will satisfy the demand of society for revenge. Neither deterrence nor retribution requires anything of the criminal. Perhaps that is why most places have lost patience with rehabilitation and do not even pretend any more that it is the rationale for how criminals are treated. That is why you will have to assume primary responsibility for your own rehabilitation. No one else can or will do it. You can get off the merry-go-round or out of the revolving door any time you want to. In this sense, your future is in your hands as it has always been.

There is no future in a life of crime. You were put on this earth for a higher, larger purpose than destroying yourself, living as a criminal, and hurting and disappointing the people who love you. If you have completed your sentence, this may be your last opportunity to "turn right, and go straight." It is up to you—not your spouse, parents, friends, girlfriend, boyfriend, or the state.

Rehabilitation consists of "any means taken to change an offender's character, habits, or behavior patterns so as to diminish his or her criminal propensities."[18] In addition to the good that is supposed to be accomplished for the prisoner when rehabilitation is taken seriously, it is also a particular mode of crime control whose goal is "to alter the offender so he or she is less inclined to offend again." The best indication of the effectiveness of "treatment programs" is the impact they have on "reducing recidivism."[19]

The usual treatment options that are used to achieve rehabilitation are "psychiatric therapy, counseling, vocational training…and behavior modification techniques."[20] In an effort to live within increasingly tight budgets, the position of chaplain has been eliminated or made part-time in some institutions. This means that you may have lots of help from mental health professionals, but little or no spiritual guidance from members of the clergy who focus more on "regeneration than rehabilitation."

By the foregoing definitions of rehabilitation, it is necessary to distinguish between what the state does to achieve it and the help that is offered to assist an offender in dealing "with his or her own problem." Ordinarily, the offender can not be coerced to accept help that he or she believes is not in his or her best interest. He or she has to be motivated to want to change and its impetus must come from within rather than from without the prisoner.

But when rehabilitation is viewed as a means of crime control or prevention designed to change the individual so that the likelihood that he or she will commit additional crimes is reduced, it may very well lead to coercion. In this situation, forcing a person into a rehabilitation treatment program is not necessarily excluded because the state's main objective is to protect the public and not to help the criminal. Another factor is that large numbers of people who are behind bars suffer from mental problems. They may not be able to choose what is in their best interest. Sometimes a little paternalism will go a long way. Some of the best things that ever happened to me came because I was made to do something I did not want to do. That was true, for example, of courses I took in school I could not see far enough ahead to realize I needed, but that prepared me for opportunities. Another example is being made to mediate cases I did not want to mediate. As a result, I got so interested in mediation that I became a mediator and an arbitrator.

For some, leaving prison depends upon going through the "state's restoration process" conducted by the parole board "for consideration for supervised release." As Dr. Karl Menninger observed years ago, there is little time for the Board to give adequate consideration to each prisoner's situation. Some asked some or all of the following questions:

"Do you think you have learned your lesson?"
"Do you intend to go straight now?"
"Will you behave yourself?"
"Can you keep out of trouble?"
"Are you sorry for what you did?"
 "Do you pray?"
"Do you have a job?"[21]

Obviously, a person who has been behind bars will say whatever he or she thinks his or her inquisitors want to hear. The problem, as Dr. Karl Menninger, the renowned psychiatrist, has observed, is that these questions are not likely to provide sufficient information for an informed judgment to be made on whether the person has been rehabilitated.[22] Although the answers to these questions may not give enough grounds for the Board to accurately predict who will succeed on parole, their basic thrust is in the right direction. They elicit evidence of change, discipline, contrition, spirituality, and employability. All of these are important indicators of your fitness for release and provide a good reason for you to work harder on yourself while you are behind bars, regardless of the decision of the Parole Board.

If your crime involved violence, especially against a police officer, your chances of obtaining early release through parole from the state parole board, are slim to none. The reasons are opposition from law enforcement organizations and politicians who are afraid of the consequences of releasing violent prisoners. In New York, for example, violent felons are attempting to address the problem through litigation that claims a constitutional violation because the Board based its decision only on the severity of the crime instead of also considering, as the law in New York requires, "the degree of remorse or rehabilitation on the likelihood that the inmate would commit another crime if released."[23] Regardless of the state where you are incarcerated, similar rules are likely to be in effect. It is incumbent upon you to learn the rules and satisfy their requirements in order to maximize your opportunity to win early release. When you do your part everybody wins. You win in the sense that you obtain an early release, and society wins by receiving a person who is less likely to re-offend.

The difficulty of deciding whether a person is good or bad risk is humorously shown by Paul Lawrence Dunbar's poem entitled "The Lawyers' Ways," where he wrote:

I've been list'nin' to them lawyers
  In the court house up the street,
An' I've come to the conclusion
  That I'm most completely beat.
Fust one feller riz to argy,
  An' he boldly waded in
As he dressed the tremblin' pris'ner
  In a coat o' deep-dyed sin.
Why, he painted him all over
  In a hue o' blackest crime,
An' he smeared his reputation
  With the thickest kind o' grime,
Tell I found myself a-wond'rin',
  In a misty way and dim,
How the Lord had come to fashion
  Sich an awful man as him.
Then the other lawyer started,
  An' with brimmin', tearful eyes,
Said his client was a martyr
  That was brought to sacrifice.
An' he give to that same pris'ner
  Every blessed human grace,
Tell I saw the light o' virtue
  Fairly shinin' from his face.
Then I own ' at I was puzzled
  How sich things could rightly be;
An' this aggervatin'question
  Seems to keep a-puzzlin' me.
So, will some one please inform me,
  An' this mystery unroll ---
How an angel an' a devil
  Can persess the self-same soul?[24]

This is the dilemma that everyone who deals with you is trying to figure out. Unfortunately, many people resolve it by avoiding people like you altogether. After all, it is the easy way out, regardless of how unfair it is to you.

There are good intentioned activists who are justified in wanting to change the structure of prisons and reform them. While that is probably needed, the likelihood of that happening anytime soon is remote as long as crime continues unabated. The evening news features the bloody carnage on our streets and this counteracts any lobbying for prison reform. People in the news business do not say "if it bleeds, it leads" for nothing. As long as people are frightened by notorious criminals, any hope of prison reform anytime soon is unrealistic.

Besides, prisoners and ex-inmates usually cannot vote. (But interestingly, they are counted for purposes of the U.S. Census to make sure the areas where they are housed receive the maximum number of federal dollars and representation in the Congress.) Their families often do not vote. If elected officials take the initiative to do anything that appears to favor prisoner rights over the interests of crime victims, they know that is political suicide. Although it is shortsighted, this is one of the reasons rehabilitation has been abandoned in favor of an approach to corrections that emphasizes punishment. It is rare for a politician to see rehabilitation as a crime prevention or public safety strategy. Doing anything that appears to be "coddling criminals" is "the kiss of death" to any one who aspires to run for or stay in public office. There are not many politicians who will demonstrate the qualities that will get them included in any edition of "Profiles in Courage." Consequently, do not hold your breath until they do something to help you. Writing them to ask for help or complain about prison conditions is usually a waste of time. Lord help them if they help you get out of prison and you rape or kill someone. Remember Willie Horton? His criminal activity on a furlough from prison contributed to the defeat of former Massachusetts Governor Michael Dukakis for the Presidency. What he did still haunts politicians—and keeps them from taking a chance on helping people like you. It is far more politically expedient to listen to those who say "lock them up and throw away the key" by building more prisons than to take a chance on people like you. There are not many Genarlow Wilsons (the young man who had consensual sex as a seventeen-year-old with a fifteen-year-old and received a ten-year prison sentence). People of all races railed against this injustice and several politicians lobbied for his release. Through the combination of these forces and the persistence of his family and lawyer, he was eventually released.

Although there is a dispute about how much effect it has, it is well documented that a reduction in crime is related to "increased reliance on prisons" to deal with the ever increasing number of violent felons. The argument is that the more people who are locked up for long periods of time, the greater the impact on the rate of crime. Although it costs $25,000.00 a year to imprison a person and there are embarrassing racial disparities in the people who are in prison,[25] the relationship between incarceration and a reduction in crime means that we are not likely to see a "moratorium" on building jails and prisons any time soon. One of the most eminent authorities in the United States, James Q. Wilson, was quoted as saying, "The typical criminal commits from 12 to 16 crimes a year" and "states that sent a higher fraction of convicts to prison had lower rates of crime." The evidence is overwhelming from a statistical perspective that deterrence is a viable theory of punishment and that increasing the risk of punishment lowers the crime rate.[26]

But not every one in jail or prison is there because of the commission of a violent felony or some other serious offense. No legitimate purpose is served by locking up "petty offenders." The irony is that it may convert them into "hardened criminals" through their forced association with "career criminals," adversely affect black families, and limit career options.[27]

There are inevitable shifts in public sentiments on how to deal with crime and criminals. Driven largely by cost considerations, get-tough policies that resulted in a prison-building binge to house ever increasing numbers of prisoners are being modified or abandoned. The pendulum is swinging back towards rehabilitation.

At least at the federal level, attitudes are changing about what to do with the large prison population in the United States. This is shown by two developments. The first is a new emphasis on prisoner reentry. Through his book, *But they all Come Back: Facing the Challenges of Prisoner Reentry*,[28] Jeremy Travis is widely credited with helping set in motion the policy changes that led the United States Congress to pass the Second Chance Act and allocate $165 million dollars to fund programs to study the problem of prisoner reentry and implement programs that facilitate this process. This law recognized the point made by Jeremy Travis, that virtually everyone who is imprisoned eventually comes back to his or her community of origin.

The second shift is in federal law on how the sentencing disparity between crack and powder cocaine has been addressed. Consequently, many people, largely African Americans, who received long prison sentences, became eligible for significant reductions in their sentences and in some instances early release because of the time they have already served. But as of this time, the law still has not been changed – despite support by the United States Justice Department and President Barack Obama, at least during his campaign.

Meanwhile, state and local governments are still straining under an extremely heavy financial burden because their jails and prisons are bulging with inmates. It is only a matter of time before the change that is underway in the federal system reaches the states. Taxpayers are at the point of revolting against paying for the warehousing of their fellow human beings and demanding a return to fiscal sanity. It is not because they think you are entitled to a break or are any less afraid of crime. Rather, it is about how much it costs to lock you up and grave concerns about the effectiveness of "get tough" policies. People are tired of crime and the cost of government.

What all of this means to you is that the climate is better now than it has been in decades for you to get job training and other help in making the transition from prison to your home community. Since opportunities will be available long before you are released, one of the best things you can do for yourself and your family is investigate what is available and do whatever is necessary to take advantage of what is offered. But remember that a job or job training alone will not keep you out of trouble. Nothing less than a radical reorientation of your life can do it. It begins by reading books like this one which help you get yourself together mentally, socially, and spiritually.

The major premise of this book is that while change may be needed, the side of the equation that is most likely to be changed is the prisoner's. That is the only side that prisoners and ex-inmates can do anything about or have control over. Regrettably, many people waste their time trying to change everyone except themselves. Family members can not change their children, spouses, or other relatives once their character is damaged through conduct that gets them convicted. If their parenting has been inadequate or their children have ignored their counsel, what happens after a conviction is up to the person behind bars. Every now and then a persistent family can get a person who was wrongly convicted a new trial and an acquittal. But that is exceedingly difficult and may not always happen despite their best effort and how much they believe in their child. In any case, the person who has the greatest opportunity to effect change is the person who was convicted. If reform occurs, it is more likely to be individual instead of institutional. But that is how the problem was created—one person at a time, not en masse. In the end, an individual approach is likely to produce the best long term results. Each one of you has an interest in rehabilitation—your liberty. The state does, too. State and federal officials are pulling for you because of their interest in lower costs, less taxes, and long term security. The exception may be managers of and investors in private prisons. In some states so many people are locked up that the burden on taxpayers is almost unbearable. For good reasons, people are afraid of crime—and those who commit it. Until you decide crime does not pay, society will keep building jails and prisons and hiring more police officers.

I know someone is asking, "What makes you think that people who have been losers all their lives and have never assumed responsibility for anything will be up to a challenge of this magnitude?" My answer is that when they think about it and are "touched by the better angels" of their nature they will realize that this is the only hope they have of a better life. The state, with all its vast resources, has not been able to do it. I believe that in the matter of personal transformation, the individual is more powerful than anything the state can bring to bear on his or her situation. I believe you and others in your predicament will not "keep doing the same things the same way and expect a different result" because you are not insane.

Prisoners, their families, and supporters often complain that prisons warehouse human beings and that the goal of rehabilitation has been abandoned. That is true. But it requires the cooperation of people who commit crimes and cannot be done without it. Just because the state has given up on a person does not mean he or she should give up on him or herself.

If a person honestly thinks or believes imprisonment is the result of racism, it is stupid to put him or herself in a position to be exploited by a system that is considered racist by continuing to break the law. By this standard, being a recidivist is just plain DUMB! The best policy is to avoid trouble at all costs. A prison population is a valuable commodity for job-starved communities everywhere, but especially in rural areas that compete for public and private jails as if they were industrial plants. Angela Y. Davis contends that "jails are designed to break human beings, to convert the population to specimen in a zoo—obedient to our keepers, but dangerous to each other."[29] Whether that is true depends upon the prisoners. This kind of dehumanization cannot occur without their consent and cooperation.

A few well meaning judges talk about doing everything they can do to make you a better person. But no judge can do that. Only you can do it. If you do not rehabilitate yourself, no one else can or will do it. No one is going to save you, but you. People who think that a jail is going to rehabilitate a person are just as misguided as those who think schools alone will educate children. If a child does not show up ready, willing and able to learn, he or she will not get an education. Nor will a person be rehabilitated who does not put forth the same effort. Prisons and jails are necessary alternatives for people who can not discipline themselves. Despite the control they exert on the lives of people who are committed to them, they cannot change a recalcitrant person. Further, the paternalism that is inherent in the process is no more likely to work in a prison setting than it has in social welfare programs in the outside world. John Ruskin was right: "Let us reform our schools, and we shall find little reform needed in our prisons."[30] The best programs and schools can do is give people the tools that are necessary to rebuild or turn their lives around. They have to do the work!

The facts of the United States Supreme Court's decision in Gall v. United States,[31] which was decided December 10, 2007, illustrate what is possible when an accused person takes responsibility for his or her conduct and voluntarily rehabilitates himself or herself.

Brian Michael Gall got involved in a conspiracy to distribute a controlled substance known as "ecstasy" when he was in college, but withdrew from the criminal enterprise after seven months, did not sell any illegal drugs after he withdrew, has not used illegal drugs, and has worked regularly since his graduation from college. Three years after he got out of the drug distribution conspiracy, he pleaded guilty to his role. Instead of prison, he received thirty-six months probation despite a pre-sentence report that recommended thirty to thirty-seven months behind bars. In upholding the U. S. District Court's departure from sentencing guidelines, the Supreme Court took note of its finding that:

> A month or two after joining the conspiracy, Gall stopped using ecstasy. A few months after that…he advised…co-conspirators that he was withdrawing from the conspiracy. He has not done illegal drugs of any kind since…He graduated from the University of Iowa in 2002, and moved first to Arizona, where he obtained a job in the construction industry, and later to Colorado, where he earned $18 per hour as a master carpenter. He has not used any illegal drugs since graduation from college.

> After Gall moved to Arizona, he was approached by federal law enforcement agents who questioned him about his involvement in the ecstasy distribution conspiracy. Gall admitted his limited participation in the distribution of ecstasy and the agents took no further action at that time. When he received notice of his indictment, Gall moved back to Iowa and surrendered to authorities. While free on his own recognizance, Gall started his own business in the construction industry, primarily engaged in sub-contracting for the installation of windows and doors. In his first year, his profits were over $2000 per month.

> . . . In her pre-sentence report, the probation officer concluded that Gall had no significant history; that he was not an organizer, leader or manager; and that his offense did not involve the use of any weapons. The report stated that Gall had truthfully provided the government with all of the evidence he had…

The record of the sentencing hearing… includes a "small flood" of letters from Gall's parents and other relatives, his fiancé, neighbors, and representatives of firms doing business with him, uniformly praising his character and work ethic.[32]
On this record, the District Court concluded:

> Any term of imprisonment in this case would be counter effective by depriving society of the contributions of the Defendant who, the court has found, understands the consequences of his criminal conduct and is doing everything in his power to forge a new life. The Defendant's post-offense conduct indicates neither that he will return to criminal behavior nor that the Defendant is a danger to society. In fact, the Defendant's post-offense conduct was not motivated by a desire to please the court or any other governmental agency, but was the pre-indictment product of the Defendant's own desire to lead a better life.[33]

In upholding the District Court's departure from the sentencing guidelines, the Supreme Court declared:

> The District Court has reasonably attached great weight to Gall's self-motivated rehabilitation, which was undertaken not at the direction of, or under supervision by, any court, but on his own initiative. This also lends strong support to the conclusion that imprisonment was not necessary to deter Gall from engaging in future conduct or to protect the public from his former criminal acts.[34]

From every indication, Gall successfully "self rehabilitated" himself.[35] That's what I am talking about!

What happened to Michael Vick is also instructive. He was sentenced to twenty-three months in prison, five months more than the district attorney agreed to recommend when Vick agreed to plead guilty to his role in a dog fighting operation because the judge concluded that he had not only failed to "fully" accept responsibility for his crime, but also lied about the level of his involvement in killing dogs and was caught smoking marijuana while he was out on bail.[36]

What can you learn from the experiences of Michael Gall and Michael Vick? At a minimum, the lesson taught by these men is that lying and not taking responsibility will get "the book" thrown at you. On the other hand, telling the truth and accepting responsibility may cause the judge to "cut you some slack." These reactions are a matter of character. In the end, good character traits like telling the truth, as evidenced in the difference in the way Gall and Vick handled adversity, trump bad character traits such as lying.

The dogs taken from the property owned by Michael Vick were described as "some of the most aggressively trained pit bulldogs in the country." Some of them had "scars and injuries appearing to be related to dog fighting." At first, these dogs were not considered "candidates to be rehabilitated," and were likely to be "put down" when they were no longer needed as "evidence," because they are not adoptable even by the standards of Humane Society officials.[37] The only exceptions were dogs that pass a behavior test administered by certified animal behaviorists from the American Society for the Prevention of Cruelty to Animals. Interestingly, each dog was evaluated rather than assumed to be dangerous because of its breed or prior training. The consensus of opinion was that only 10 to 20 percent of them had the potential to be "rehabilitated." Only after each dog was evaluated was a decision made on its fate. But at the end of this process, all of the dogs were spared except one.[38] A lot of people do not get this kind of individual attention. More often than not, they are lumped into a sack and treated in accordance with preconceived ideas about them. If it is unfair to pit bulldogs to judge them except on an individual basis, it is definitely unfair to you or any one else with a bad reputation. But who said life is fair?

Under the best of circumstances, pit bulldogs have a bad "reputation." But those that have been trained to be even more vicious than they are by nature are probably held in even lower esteem. The conventional wisdom was that no right thinking person would ever take one of these dogs as a family pet, because the risks are too great that it will maim or kill someone. When the screening and "rehabilitation" process was completed, all of the dogs that were saved were eventually adopted. So much for conventional wisdom!

While human beings with prison records are not in the same category as pit bulldogs, they are likely to be regarded the same way—especially if they committed a violent crime. The irony is that research has consistently shown that murderers, for example, are much less likely to re-offend than criminals who commit other crimes. Sexual predators, especially pedophiles, are in another category. They are, rightly or wrongly, almost universally regarded as beyond hope.

As the options for "unrehabilitated" pit bulldogs are permanent confinement or destruction, in the minds of many people in society, that is how a person in your position should be treated. Many people think pit bulldogs that have been trained to fight have a better chance to be rehabilitated than you. They just do not think you can be rehabilitated. Your challenge is to prove them wrong—just as Vick's pitbulls did. On this question you will always bear the burden of proof.

Ordinarily in dog bite cases, a dog is entitled to one bite before its dangerous propensity is legally established. In that case the owner of the dog is on notice and is liable for any subsequent injury or damage his or her dog causes. For many of you, your conviction is the "bite" that proves dangerousness and provides proof positive of what you will do because we have learned that "the best way to predict what a person will do is what he has done."

Isaac Watts calls us to a higher standard than any animal is capable of meeting in these words:

Let dogs delight to bark and bite,
For God hath made them so;
Let bears and lions growl and fight;
For 'tis their nature too . . .
But children you should never let
Such angry passions rise,

Your little hands were never made
To tear each other's eyes.[39]

Because you are not a dog, bear or lion, there is hope for you. When you realize who you are as a human being and child of God, rehabilitation will be within your reach.

None of what I say in this book is intended to suggest that you are the sole cause of all of your problems. That is an entirely different question than the question of who is responsible for fixing them. There may very well be lots of people and institutions beyond your control that contributed to the making of the person you have become such as parents who did not parent, schools that did not educate, and churches that did not nurture. The nature of a system indicates that we are impacted by what others do that we are in relationship with. I have no doubt that your wholeness and rehabilitation may well depend upon how well you deal with them. But if you spend the rest of your life blaming people or looking for sympathy instead of doing what you can to change your life, your situation is hopeless! Lots of people overcome bad circumstances, including grinding poverty and single parent homes without becoming or remaining criminals. Few people are going to feel sorry for you. You had the same opportunity to make something out of yourself that every one else had. You might as well make your reservations now for your return to prison if you do not change your thinking. The best indication that you are ready to make the best of your new beginning is an attitude that accepts responsibility for overcoming whatever may have caused your problems instead of blaming everybody else because regardless of what your circumstances were, they could not have gotten you where you are without your complete cooperation! It might not have always been knowing and intentional, but it was your cooperation that got you where you are. All blaming some one else for your problems does is delay the time when you "get your act together" by assuming responsibility for solving your problem. When I did an internship as a group leader in an alcohol rehabilitation clinic years ago, I noticed that the people who did the best in overcoming alcoholism were those who accepted responsibility for their drinking. The ones who did the worst were always blaming their spouse, employer, or anyone else for their alcoholism. The best indication that they were getting better was their acceptance of responsibility for their behavior. It might have been caused by somebody else, but when they cooperated by over reacting or not having enough discipline to "just say no" or "walk away," it became theirs—and so it was and is with you. In prison this is construed as weakness, and so often inmates get into fights that they lose in order to obtain respect. What worked in prison does not work in conventional society. If you are going to stay out of trouble outside of prison, you cannot resolve conflicts through fights.

Somebody is depending on you to make good. It could be a son, daughter, father, mother, grandparent or spouse. The last thing they need is for you to let them down! It is time for you to realize that your lifestyle hurts not only you, but the people who love you. They have suffered enough because you have not gotten your act together. What follows is offered to help you get yourself together and do what is necessary to leave prison, this time for good.

CHAPTER TWO
Personal Transformation through Spiritual Rebirth

In making or attempting to make changes in one's personal life, it is important to realize that as important as human effort is, it is grossly inadequate. Most of you know that: you are not where you are because you have not tried to get yourself together. The problem for many people is that their inner strength has not been sufficient to contend with the temptation to do wrong. As one of my clients put it years ago, "I was going down the street, minding my own business and up jumped the devil." The object of this chapter is to help you become a new person through reliance upon and transformation by a power that is greater than anything you can muster on your own through new resolutions, or good intentions. That power is spiritual rather than carnal. It alone makes it possible for a person to consistently say no to evil.

2.1 SPIRITUALITY

Recreate Yourself

As women make themselves over with new hairdos and wardrobes, you can make yourself over by discovering spirituality. The "mental make over" that will allow you to recreate yourself begins with recognition of the fact that the only person you can change is yourself. Beliefs, values, and attitudes determine not only who you are, but also how you behave. The only way to change either is to change your attitude, values, and beliefs.[1] This is probably the most difficult thing you will ever undertake. Not only is it difficult, it is also painful.

Doing it by yourself, "cold turkey," is probably not going to be successful. People who have done it almost always need some supernatural help. What is virtually impossible in the flesh, becomes readily doable in the spirit. The power of the Holy Spirit is activated through the practice of such spiritual disciplines as prayer and Bible Study. That is the secret to successfully recreating yourself. The experiences of people of different faith traditions prove this point. Malcolm X, for example, was a "petty criminal" before his conversion to Islam and emergence as a "voice for black empowerment."[2] St. Augustine was preoccupied with "cheap entertainment and sex"[3] before his life was transformed and he became "a father of the Catholic Church." What these men have in common with you and most other people who change their lifestyle is that they reached a "low point" in their lives. When this happened they realized that they needed to change.[4] This seems to require a person to reach what counselors call "rock bottom."

If you realize that your old attitude, beliefs, and values are keeping you from becoming the person you were meant to be, it may mark the beginning of a spiritual awakening that has put you in touch with a power greater than anything you have ever experienced before. If the adversity you are going through has this effect on you, it may be the best thing that ever happened to you.

Learn The Secret of Personal Transformation

Almost everyone who ends up in jail or prison identifies himself or herself as a Christian. The exception is, according to an old joke, the fellow who, when asked if he was a Christian, said no, "I am a Baptist." Regardless of their denominational affiliation, the predicament of people in prison gives evidence that they were probably never converted. Perhaps that is why many became open to a deeper faith in God only after their incarceration.

William James, the founder of modern psychology, saw a positive side of hopelessness. He observed that people tend to have a conversion experience in response to it. When they are at a low point in their lives they give up and become open to divine revelation. When this happens, they become less egotistical than before and begin to live their lives for others as a "higher goal."[5]

Dependence upon God results in the ability to face life without fear, and this courage and total security in God are the source of converts' motivation to give up things and make sacrifices that were previously unimaginable. This process leads to total transformations that are manifested in an attitudinal shift that involves total willingness to "leave the self behind in the cause of something greater" such as God or country, living in conformity to "larger forces, laws, or designs," and the ability to see the "higher part of them as their real self, and also to leave their lower self behind."[6]

For good reasons, people are often skeptical of jail house conversions. But some of the most authentic conversions have occurred as a result of a prison experience. The example of Charles Colson comes to mind. He always struck me as pompous and arrogant when he served in the Nixon administration. But he became a new man when he was "born again."

Get Control of Yourself

The Apostle Paul had a lot to say about self-control and the lack of it. On one occasion he said he did not understand himself. He could make up his mind to do right but could not do it. In fact, the very thing he resolved that he would not do was what he did. Does this sound familiar? Paul found that the answer to his problem was reliance on the power of the Holy Spirit. (See Romans 7:14f)

One of the most prolific writers on self control is Napoleon Hill. For him, it is the "ability to direct your thoughts and thus your actions, in pursuit of your definite chief aim." He argues that all those who have it, not only are successful in reaching their goals, but also are those "which the world calls great."[7] Self-control is such a powerful determinant of success because everything we do involves people and it has such potential to negatively impact the relationships that we need to reach our goals in sales, job promotions, romantic interests, and virtually everything else that is worthwhile. If you will think about it, it will be readily apparent that the people who make decisions about which people to hire, date, promote, or give other benefits to, are more likely to favor someone they like rather than someone who acts like a horse's behind or regularly flies off the handle at the slightest real or imagined provocation. As you can see, as Hill argued, the person who is hurt the most by your lack of self-control is you!

Although it is never easy, the greatest test of your faith, if any, and your character is likely to be how you handle sexual desires while you are imprisoned. It cannot be done without self-discipline, which is a matter of controlling yourself. God gives you the power to do it. But you have to exercise it if you are going to survive incarceration with your health, dignity, and manhood (or womanhood, if you are a female) intact. An elderly lady told me she kept her sons out of trouble by telling them if they got locked up somebody in prison would try to "put a dress on them." The "convict code," which dictates that you avoid the appearance of weakness in order to prevent homosexual rape involves willingness to fight, even if you lose, so that fellow inmates will respect you. In other words, fighting is perceived to be the only way to keep someone from "putting a dress" on you. A lot of you will not trust guards to protect you and will take the law into your own hands as you did on the streets, regardless of the consequences. But the citizenship skills that are needed to survive in society are the same ones that should be practiced in prison. At a minimum, that means respecting the rule of law.

If your community of origin is like most places, sex was readily available. Whatever appetite you had could be satisfied with virtual impunity. With loosened morals, and growing acceptance of what used to be regarded as immoral, almost anything goes now. The constraints that used to exist are, for the most part, gone. As long as you did not rape anybody, the sex was consensual, and the sexual partner was of age, everything was all right. At one time, one's partner had to be of the right race and of the opposite sex. But today none of these issues matter. About all a person needs to worry about is the age of the person who is propositioned, police stings for prostitution, and not catching "a case" of some kind of sexually transmitted disease.

Adding to the moral laxity and confusion of sexual identity of the times is the phenomenon known as the "down low." In the minds of some people, it is a direct result of the life style and sexual practices of former inmates and the values of hip hop culture. Under its cover, there are people who regularly engage in homosexual activity, but do not consider themselves gay. They may, in fact, have girlfriends who are none the wiser because from every outward appearance their man is "straight." There are some who are openly gay and some who are transsexuals. As a pastor, I hold that they are no less favored by God than any other sinner and are therefore in need of the salvation that is offered through Jesus to all of us. Aren't you glad that God loves sinners?

You will undoubtedly face the same sexual temptations in prison that are part of the culture, with greatly reduced opportunities to satisfy them. While the setting where you will serve your sentence will have people of all "persuasions," indulging your passions in prison carries a set of penalties and risks that are serious enough that if you have half a brain you will exercise restraint until you are reunited with your spouse, or you do the right thing and get married. Don't you expect your spouse or fiancé to remain abstinent while you are behind bars? What used to be dismissed as old fashioned values that are irrelevant to how real people live are now a matter of life and death. Without becoming indelicate, even a superficial cost-benefit analysis will lead all but the most hedonistic, irresponsible, or stupid to the conclusion that living temporarily without sex is far better than living permanently with HIV or AIDS. Moreover, if you sexually assault or rape someone, you may face not only criminal prosecution, but also swift justice of the self-help variety that you may not survive even though you are in prison for a noncapital offense. In a real sense, the choice in this matter is between life and death, as it is with every other aspect of your lifestyle. Do not expect anyone to feel sorry for you if you are maimed or killed because you sexually assaulted someone in prison. By the same token, if you are maimed or killed in self defense while you are attempting to rape someone, a lot of people will say good riddance! That is why you have to avoid behavior that hurts others or will get you hurt or killed! Just think how any kind of crime in prison will be viewed by a judge and jury, especially something as odious as homosexual rape. If a prison record is not bad enough, just imagine how a sexual assault behind bars will play with a potential employer if you ever get out of prison. If you are serious about getting out of prison alive and doing something useful with your life anytime soon, the last thing you need is another sentence for another crime or record of discipline for any kind of sexual misconduct.

How you handle sexual temptation is a severe test of your ability not only to make responsible decisions, but also to control yourself. Your future as a husband, wife, father, or mother when you return to your family may turn on this decision. Your family should not have to relive your bad decisions. Nowhere is that more likely or dangerous than in the matter of sex.

If you cannot control yourself under the circumstances you are in now, with guards and fellow inmates watching, what will you do the first time you come in contact with a member of the opposite sex when you get out of prison? The stories of men whose advances were rejected by former girlfriends and led to rape or assault charges are numerous. No means no! Failure to understand that will result in your re-imprisonment. Failure to control yourself may limit visits by well meaning volunteers of the same or opposite sex out of fear that they will be sexually assaulted. If this happens, it will severely limit opportunities for you to get the spiritual and vocational counseling you need to transition from prison to life on the outside. Before leaving this sensitive subject, let me give you some strategies for dealing with the issue of sex.

Napoleon Hill wrote a lot of books on how to be successful and get rich. In Think and Grow Rich, he explains at length the role of "sex transmutation" in this process.

By transmuting he means "the changing, or transferring of one element or form of energy, into another."

He talks about the effect of sex on one's mind, and calls what he describes "the emotion of sex," which "brings into being a state of mind." He rejects the idea that sex is as much a physical phenomenon as we have made it. What he calls "the emotion of sex" can be used for three constant purposes:

The perpetuation of mankind.
The maintenance of health.
The transformation of mediocrity into genius through transmutation.[8]

As applied to sex, transmutation is "switching of the mind from thoughts of physical expression, to thoughts of some other nature." Hill acknowledges that "sex desire is the most powerful of human desire." As he explains it:

When driven by this desire, men develop keenness of imagination, courage, will power, persistence, and creative ability unknown to them at other times. So strong and impelling is the desire for sexual contact that men freely run the risk of life and reputation to indulge it. When harvested and redirected along other times, this motivating force maintains all its attributes of keenness of imagination, courage, etc., which may be used as powerful creative forces in literature, art, or in any other profession or calling, including, of course, the accumulation of riches.[9]

What Hill calls transmutation requires great "will power" or "self-control." He says,"the desire for sexual expression is inborn and natural. The desire cannot and should not be submerged or eliminated. But it should be given an outlet through forms of expressions which enrich the body, mind and spirit of man. If not given this form of outlet, through transmutation, it will seek outlets through purely physical channels."[10]

One of the more interesting things Hill says is that people rarely become successful until they reach the age of forty and that their "greatest capacity to create" occurs "between forty and sixty." In his view, the reason is that "man begins to learn (if he ever learns) the art of sex transmutation" between the age of thirty and forty.[11] That is why it is not too late for you to rediscover your dreams and accomplish your worthwhile goals.

Dealing with sexual urges when they cannot legally be satisfied has led many people to become successful in areas of life that they probably never thought were possible. As sexual energy is one of the strongest forces in life when it is transmuted and put to good use, it is amazing what it allows otherwise marginal and unmotivated people to accomplish. This thought is an important part of the teaching of Napoleon Hill who incorporated it into his exploration of the "science of success."[12]

A second strategy for dealing with sex is suggested by Mahatma Gandhi, the Hindu political and spiritual leader. It is not widely known that Gandhi, the source of inspiration for Dr. Martin Luther King's non-violent tactics which led to the transformation of American society, was married at age thirteen. This apparently caused him to be dogged by shame, which was complicated by a sense of guilt over lust. He started to believe that sex was not for the satisfaction of fleshly desire, but to have children, which, incidentally, is the classic view of many Christians, especially Catholics. When he was in his mid-thirties, with his wife's consent, he made a vow of celibacy called brah macharya, which he attributed to his "flowering as a human being." The meaning of brah macharya is "control of the senses in thought, word, and deed, especially sexually, in search of self-purification which will lead one to God." Although he admitted that this was difficult, he eventually got to a point where "lust no longer had control over his thinking" and he could value the vow's purpose of "protecting a person's body, mind, and soul."[13] Unless you are in a facility that allows conjugal visits by spouses, the experience of Gandhi may be instructive on how to handle the challenge of state and self-imposed celibacy during your incarceration. Two biblical examples you should study are Paul (see 1Corinthians 7) and Joseph (Genesis 39:1-20 NKJV).

The Apostle Paul recognized the danger of lust. For him the antidote to this problem was living in the spirit (Gal. 5:16-26). This, of course, only comes for a Christian through a relationship with Jesus who gave us the Holy Spirit to be our comforter and guide (John 14:16 NKJV).

Prisons were originally conceived as a place that promoted penitence and remorse. That is seen in the use of the word penitentiary. In the early years of their existence they were built around monasteries or churches. This underscores the power of the early belief that crime and the people who commit crimes cannot be dealt with without the powerful influence of spirituality. No other force can do as much to help broken people make sense of life and become whole. There is an inseparable connection between spirituality and dealing with the consequences of criminal conduct. When I speak of spirituality, I refer to the process of getting in touch and connecting with the supernatural power that is only available through a relationship with God. I realize that, for some, God may be known by another name —or referred to as a higher power.

The work of exorcizing various demons—yours, or those you inherited from your family—is one of the most urgent tasks that you can undertake. It cannot be done successfully without the benefit of the spiritual resources that are available to you from your faith tradition. Some of your demons can only be "cast out," according to Jesus, by "fasting and prayer" (St. Matt. 17:21 NKJV). (Caveat: Before undertaking a fast, be sure there is no medical contraindication for it by getting medical advice before you start).

In the spirit, there are no limits to what you can do.

You can be transported to faraway places—and accomplish superhuman feats of strength and scholarship. Further, it is the only way to make sure you behave yourself. If you walk in the spirit, Paul says, you shall not fulfill the lust of the flesh" (Gal. 5:16 NKJV). Only in the spirit can you become the person you were meant to be because your will, passion, and thoughts are brought under the control of a power that is greater than anything that is available to you in the flesh. In the spirit, you can be happy and feel good without mind altering drugs. The word enthusiasm means "in God."

When God is in you, there is nothing you cannot do. No wonder Jesus said, "for without me you can do nothing" (St. John 15:5 NKJV). For Christians, the answer to failure and futility is Jesus. For people of other faith traditions, there are other answers to this problem. Whatever path you choose, it is important to be faithful in following its precepts if it is going to do you any good.

Get Your Spiritual House in Order

One of the first and most helpful things you can do is seek a relationship with God. Bringing spiritual power to bear on your life is the single most important thing you can do to stay out of trouble—and jail or prison. The late Dr. Curtis Tolbert, who lovingly doled out advice to generations of young inmates, often said "get some sense in your head, some money in your pocket, and some God in your heart." Having said that, you need to know that people are skeptical of jailhouse conversions and "jailhouse religion." While all of us know people who had a miraculous religious conversion that turned their lives around forever, there are plenty of ex-inmates who used religion for the wrong reason and reverted to their old life style as soon as their feet hit "terra firma." The folk in the latter category are ones who are the most likely to end up back in jail or prison—and give "jailhouse religion" a bad name.

When a person is converted, his or her life is under new management. Most of you have messed up everything you have put your hands on. This may be the time for you to start to "walk by faith and not sight" by learning to live in the power of the Holy Spirit. It begins when you invite Jesus into your life, repent of your sins, accept the forgiveness of God, and trust in somebody other than yourself—God. The Word of God teaches that "if anyone is in Christ, he is a new creation (II Cor. 5:17 NKJV); and that a person is trans-formed by the 'renewing' of his mind" (Rom. 12:2 NKJV). There is a lot of guilt associated with bad decisions. But the good news, as the Bible says, is that, "There is therefore now no condemnation to those who are in Christ Jesus, who do not walk after the flesh, but according to the Spirit" (Rom. 8:1 NKJV).

Too often people with "issues" excuse themselves by saying, "That's just the way I am!" Some say, "I was born that way." The biblical answer to this response is that is why you need to be "born again" (St. John 3:3 NKJV). That is the answer to bad conduct, regardless of whether its cause is "nature or nurture."

Get Fit

One of the ironies of incarceration is that after you are removed from society for an extended period of time, you are expected to know how to reintegrate yourself back into the community you came from and get along with others as if nothing has happened. This situation is made worse if your period of imprisonment included any significant amount of solitary confinement. The skills we need to relate to other "normal" human beings must be practiced with enough frequency for us to stay in touch with our own humanity. Coming out of prison means, at a minimum, that you have to work on the social and people skills you will need when you are released. This is an important reason that you should not burn your bridge to your community of origin. Being reconciled with family members and the right kind of friends is essential because visits and letters from them will give you the opportunity to stay connected with your community and practice the people and social skills you will need. Reading the newspaper from your hometown will also help.

As important as all of these steps are, the most important work is making yourself fit for reintegration into your community of origin or any other place you choose to live. That begins when you become "fit for yourself to know." If you adopt a good set of absolute values instead of trying to live as if values are relative, you can make it anywhere. No one can do this for you. Others can help you by lovingly holding you accountable and not enabling you to engage in irresponsible behavior, but you must do the heavy lifting.

The best source of help you can get with this task is spiritual. Regardless of the nature of your crime, you will always be an ex-inmate in the eyes of people who know you and the people you seek help or employment from, possibly for the rest of your life. Whether that limits you or becomes a stepping stone is up to you. With God's help you can rise above your mistake and go on to something useful and worthwhile. That is done every time a person is genuinely converted. I do not mean the game that some ex-inmates run with the weak, immature faith they used to have. I am talking about the kind of radical reorientation of your life which occurs when you turn away from old habits and ways of behaving and live in accordance with the principles of God's word through the power of the Holy Spirit. That only happens when you surrender your life to God by accepting a relationship with his son, Jesus Christ. The Bible teaches that "if you confess with your mouth the Lord Jesus and believe in your heart that God hath raised Him from the dead, you will be saved" (Rom. 10:9 NKJV). The kind of lip service religion you used to have did not do you any good. The kind of religion I am talking about will make you a new person. Some will think they need a new faith. But if you do not do any better with it than the old one you had, it will not produce any better results in your life. It is well documented that Islam has had a profound effect on the lives of prisoners. Again, one of the best examples of the transformation it produces is the life of Malcolm X.

Because Christians may not be as likely to be involved in prison ministry or see it as an important crime prevention strategy, as members of other faiths, you may not have sufficient appreciation of the role of your faith in changing lives. For Christians, the hope of a better life is focused on Jesus. What Jesus does is make you fit for community. He did it for "the dregs of society" when he was on earth—the prostitute, demon possessed, criminals, misfits, ignorant, poor, lepers, blind, insane, deaf, lame, and even the dead. Many of you are what society now calls "dregs" that are beyond redemption. But you are just right for Jesus. While most people despise and reject folk like you, Jesus says you can come to him and promises not to reject you. When you accept this relationship something will happen to you as it did with so many over the centuries. No one else has been able to reach you. Only Jesus can open your ears so that you will be able to hear Godly counsel. One of the members of the church I pastor told me, "Pastor you are preaching better." I said, "The Lord be praised—but I am not preaching better. I am preaching the same way I've always preached. It may just be that you are hearing better." So it will be with you. Your eyes will be opened and you will be able to see opportunities where before all you could see were obstacles. By God's grace, those who once were blind will be able to see. And the lost will be found. Those of you who have been crippled by bad habits will be able to walk. Those who were dead in trespasses and sins will be raised to new life.

When Jesus works in the life of a person, he or she is so completely changed from whatever state he or she was in that it is as if a new birth has occurred. This is what he offers you. As the folk he healed were made fit for community through what he did in their lives, Jesus Christ is able to do the same for you. The most important thing you can do is invite him into your life.

What he did in the life of Paul is what he will do for you. Paul was a man who was radically converted on the road to Damascus. He was so zealous for the cause of Judaism that he did not tolerate the emergence of Christianity. He resorted to violence in order to suppress it. His behavior did not change until he was confronted by God (Acts 9:1-30). He became a Christian, wrote a significant portion of the Bible, and became a leading advocate of the faith he had tried to destroy. This is his testimony:

> For I through the law died to the law that I might live to God. I have been crucified with Christ; it is no longer I who live, but Christ lives in me; and the life which I now live in the flesh I live by faith in the Son of God, who loved me and gave Himself for me (Gal. 2:19-20 NKJV).

With a life like yours, I know it is hard to fathom the idea that God loves you. But he does! In fact, "He commended his love towards you" in that while you were yet involved in sin, Christ died for ungodly people like you and me. (Rom. 5:8)

Thank God for Prison

Am I crazy? Not at all. But if you think about it, you will agree with me. Paul said: "And we know that all things work together for good to those who love God, to those who are the called according to His purpose" (Rom. 8:28 NKJV).

If you use what you are going through, it could be the best thing that ever happened to you. How can that be? Just think of the opportunities you had to stop the progression of your life that you did not take advantage of and use to make your life better. It took jail or prison to get your attention. It was no accident. You would not have chosen this experience. No sane person sets out to be a criminal or go to jail. If he or she does, getting caught and thrown into jail is certainly not part of the plan.

The God I know is incredibly efficient. Nothing goes to waste. People who survive have learned their lesson. As black people learned to eat chitterlings, pig ears, pig feet, and almost every other part of a hog, what others throw away can sometimes be put to good use. Many African Americans have used what others threw away to build prosperous businesses. Soul food restaurants feature products that were once waste that a little creativity turned into delicacies. People coming out of jail or prison can use what others despise and throw away to not just get by, but build a better life.

In this sense, the years you are spending or spent in jail or prison are not wasted. Your head might have been so hard that it took all the time you spent behind bars to become the person you are now. God does not give "social promotions." He only allows you to move from one level to the next when you have learned the lesson he wants to teach you in order for you to succeed where he wants to put you.

Perhaps you were in jail or prison before. This time, however, will be different because now you have a chance not to be a better prisoner, but a better person. The purpose of putting gold in the fire is not to destroy it, but to refine it. God loves you too much to allow you to be destroyed by your circumstances. The object is for you to learn from your experience. When you "stop kicking against the pricks," (Acts 9:5) and surrender to God's plan for your life, your pain will subside.

State criminal justice systems are catching up with the federal system in toughness through the imposition of mandatory sentences that are designed to incarcerate certain felons for long periods of time. If you have been adjudged a serious violent offender in Georgia, for example, you have an especially difficult "row to hoe." A serious violent felony includes:

Murder or Felony Murder;
Armed Robbery
Kidnapping;
Rape;
Aggravated Child Molestation;
Aggravated Sodomy; or
Aggravated Sexual Battery

A conviction for a violent felony requires a mandatory minimum prison term of ten years, which cannot be "suspended, stayed, probated, deferred or withheld." Further, a person convicted of a serious violent felony is ineligible for sentencing as a first offender, which can have a positive effect on your record upon successful completion of the sentence.[14]

A person sentenced to life in prison must serve a minimum of fourteen years in prison. If a person was sentenced to death and the sentence was commuted to life in prison, that person must serve a minimum of twenty-five years. Any other sentence must be served in its entirety. In neither case can the sentence be reduced by earned time, early release, work release, or any other similar measure.[15]

For all of its emphasis on freedom, the United States consistently leads the world in the number of its citizens behind bars. By some estimates, 1.4 million people are in our prisons. Only seven percent are in prison with a death or life sentence. Despite all of the tough talk and harsh sentences, 93 percent of prisoners are eventually released. Many of them had an average sentence of twenty-nine months. But according to some estimates, 44 percent of all state or 27 percent of all federal prisoners have less than one year remaining to serve.[16] If you are still in prison, I hope you are in this category.

If you did not get convicted of a serious violent felony in a state like Georgia, you should thank God. But you should also pause to thank God that you saw the light before you progressed to the commission of an offense that could get you sent away for a long time—if you have seen it. You have seen it, haven't you? The next time you may not be among those who will be doing a relatively short time in prison.

Get Over Your Pain

That may be easier said than done, but it is absolutely essential. No one can do anything about your pain but you. While God's grace promotes healing and the ability to bear pain, there is something for you to do. It is essential that you understand the relationship between the pain that you feel and what others did to you, when you could not help yourself and no one came to your rescue. Dr. A. Louis Patterson observes that "people who were hurt by someone else tend to hurt other people."[17] Sometimes it is out of revenge. At other times it is imitation. Understanding this simple truth may unlock the secret of your behavioral pattern. If someone wounded you as a child or as an adult, there is, in all likelihood, a vast reservoir of anger and ill-will that supply the energy and motivation for the anti-social way you relate to other people. Success on the outside requires that this be changed. A step in the direction towards healing and wholeness begins when you come to terms with what is behind your behavior. Towards this end, the following steps should be taken:

> Honestly confront your past;
> Deal with anger in a constructive manner;
> Forgive the persons in your past who caused your pain; and
> Let go of the desire to avenge what others did to you.

Because "wounded people wound others," the first step in your restoration to society begins with your own healing. Heal your wounds, and you become less likely to inflict the wounds which you have suffered on others and end up back in prison.

The news recently featured an account of a man who killed his father. Three years before, he got into an altercation with his father which resulted in his father shooting him. He later confessed that the motive for killing his father was revenge for his father shooting him three years earlier. Obviously, he had not dealt with this issue, and it eventually caused him to commit a horrible crime.

There are people who will tell you to just get over it! I wish it was that simple. Personal healing is one of the most difficult things you will ever do; but healing your mind and your spirit can be done by the power of God. The worst thing you can do is mask your pain through the use of drugs or alcohol. All that does is make your problem worse.

Be Real

The culture emphasizes "keeping it real." That is an excuse to stoop to pretty low levels of self expression. That is not what I mean when I say be real. I mean you should be genuine or authentic.

Beware of counterfeit religion. It is a poor substitute for genuine spirituality. Religion alone will not make you a better person if you do not live by its tenets. A lot of people will not be impressed when you tell them you are "saved" when they learn that your salvation was the result of a jailhouse conversion. They are going to think this is just another scam you are pulling or game you are running—especially if you "talk the talk but do not walk the walk." I met a "trustee" at a prison several years ago who was asked about his religious background by the warden for the benefit of a group of ministers I was with who were being interviewed for a chaplaincy position. "John," he said, "You're a Christian aren't you? John replied: "Oh, yassir, yassir! In fact, I've been baptized two or three times, but didn't nan one of 'em take." Does this sound familiar? A superficial, inauthentic profession of faith will not do you any good in the long run. You may be able to fool some of the people you come in contact with, but most people can spot a phony a mile away. Besides, God knows your heart and he cannot be fooled at any time.

Any time is a good time to get right with God. But when one's conversion occurs behind bars it invites people to be cynical about it. The only way to deal with the misgivings of others is to become a genuine ambassador of the faith you profess. If that happens, your behavior will speak louder than anything you say about your new life.

Understand that Life Has More Than One Side

Balance is the key. The healthy person is able to balance work, play, and other relational interests. Whatever we spend the most time on tends to become dominant. We have two natures. Whichever one we feed the most will get the strongest. As pumping iron will result in strong muscles, study will produce strong minds. A balanced approach to life means we focus on every aspect of life. Perhaps the most neglected area is spiritual development. It is through this means that you access a source of power that is greater than anything that can be found through any other means. It is deeper than what you think or believe. Quiet reflection, meditation, Bible study and prayer are the means through which you can get it.

Understand the Difference between an Apology and Repentance

There is a big difference between the word apology and repentance. Whenever a mistake is made, the person at fault is usually quick to say "I apologize." That is true of all kinds of people. We hear apologies for all kinds of transgressions; but we never hear anyone say, I repent. A person can say he apologizes without meaning anything more than I am sorry I got caught and with little acceptance of responsibility as illustrated by those who say "if I offended anyone, I apologize." Repentance, by definition, is different. It means that you have changed your mind about specific conduct. A change in the way you think makes you far less likely to repeat the conduct than a simple apology. The story is told of a Sunday School teacher who asked a little boy to tell her the meaning of the word repent. He said it is "being sorry for what you did." A little girl added, "it is being sorry enough to quit."

We let people off the hook too quickly when they say "I apologize." The best evidence of its sincerity and intent is sorrow, contrition, unconditional acceptance of responsibility for the wrong, and a change in behavior. How many times have you heard folk apologize for the same offence? It happens over and over because it did not come from a spirit of repentance, which is a change of mind.

Only in the spirit is it possible for a person to genuinely repent because the hardest thing for any of us to do is admit we are wrong and change the way we think and behave. Your mantra should be, "I can do all things through Christ who strengthens me" (Phil. 4:13 NKJV). In the flesh you will remain arrogant and cocky. But in the power of the spirit, the humility is possible that leads to sorrow for wrongdoing, and that ultimately leads to repentance. Moral: Do not just apologize for what you have done, repent!

Don't Pray for What You Can Do Something About

Alcoholic: "I pray the Lord will take the taste of liquor out of my mouth."

Preacher: "God is not going to do that because he has placed the decision as to whether to drink under your control. You can choose to quit whenever you want to."

As important as spirituality is, it cannot do for you what you should do for yourself. In one form or another, all of us have heard that "God helps those who help themselves." That is true because the Bible reminds us that we are "workers together with Him," (II Cor. 6:1 NKJV) and that "faith by itself, if it does not have works, is dead" (James 2:17 NKJV).

There are some things you cannot pray your way out of. Even Jesus prayed unsuccessfully for deliverance from crucifixion. Paul prayed unsuccessfully for relief from a lot of pain. But as Jesus was not spared and Paul was not delivered, you may not be relieved from the consequences of the behavior that caused your imprisonment. The prayers of Jesus and Paul were not answered for a specific reason. Jesus had an unalterable mission to accomplish. Paul discovered that God's strength is made perfect in weakness and that God's grace was sufficient. Getting through your prison experience may be a similar opportunity for you to learn how to trust God and depend upon him when no one else is available to lend a helping hand. In the end, there are some things you have to go through and take care of yourself. That is what Sarah K. Bolton meant when she wrote these words:

Nothing great is lightly won,
Nothing won is lost—
Every good deed nobly done,
Will repay the cost
Leave to Heaven, in humble trust,
All you will to do;

But if you succeed, you must
Paddle your own canoe.[18]

Put Your Life to Good Use

It sounds inhumane to say people can be recycled because we think of alumi-
num cans, newspapers, cardboard, old clothes, plastic bottles, and all kinds of other
products that are reclaimed from the garbage cans of the world and reused. But to do
otherwise is to suggest that people lose all value when they obtain a criminal record.
I submit that the value of many is not discovered until after their time in jail or prison.
Some discover talents they never knew they had. Others had talent all the time, but
did not get motivated to use it in a socially acceptable way until they got locked up.
Finding a new use for your life is the key that opens all kinds of doors.

God has a lot invested in us, to say nothing of our families. Unfortunately, we
devalue people in the same way we devalue consumer products. Some things are
easier to replace than fix or use in some other way. That should not be true of people.
No one should be expendable because all of us have some value. Besides, what the
advertisement of a recycling company said of things is true of people: "It just makes
sense to use something again instead of throwing it away." I have seen people get rid
of one spouse, and because of the way they are "wired" or other psychological reasons
which they are not aware of, marry someone just like the person who was divorced. If
it was an alcoholic, they end up with another alcoholic. If it was a physically abusive
person, that is the kind of relationship they are attracted to. They would have been
better off dealing with the "devil they knew" instead of having to learn the ways of
another spouse.

The world throws you away when it can no longer use you. Because of your
value to God, he can still use you, but only after you have been changed from what
you have become into the person he wants you to be. He will not use you as you are
after you have been used up by the world. But if you let him, He will recycle you for
his purposes.

Deal with Your Demons

Some people say you need to make peace with your inner demons. I say you cannot make peace with them. You have to drive them out. If you just make peace with
the devil by conceding any part of your mind or life to his control, he will use it as a
strong hold from which to make war against you. According to history, the Japanese
pretended to seek peace during World War II. While their representatives were pretending to be preparing to talk peace, their bombers were already in the air headed for
Pearl Harbor where they wrought almost decisive havoc. The war did not end until
they were soundly defeated.

The scripture makes it clear that we are in a war against wickedness that is personi-
fied by the devil and his demons (II Cor. 10:3-4 NKJV). Their pernicious work is seen
in the destruction that was wrought on the campus of Virginia Tech, where a deranged
gunman went on a rampage that resulted in the death of several innocent people, and

in the compulsions, obsessions, drug addictions, sexual immorality, and alcoholism of many. For those with symptoms of psycho- pathology, psychiatric evaluation and treatment are necessary. But the relationship between some of this conduct and demon possession should not be discounted. In Greek, the word sorcery means "enchantment with drugs," and its root is the word from which we get the word pharmacy. From this, it can be seen that the occult is associated with drugs. In scripture, demons are responsible for physical diseases, dumbness, blindness, mental disorder, death, and perversion.

The only way the Christian tradition offers to deal with demons is exorcism which is nothing less than the binding of evil powers by means of a command direct-ly to the devil or through a prayer that God demand that he leave.[19] In this sense it is a form of spiritual healing that can restore the health of a person who is oppressed by demons.

There is growing recognition that the children of alcoholics are at increased risk of becoming alcoholics. This causes some people to talk about their father's demons or their mother's demons. While that shows insight into the origin of the problem, it does not matter whose demons you are dealing with or where they came from. If they are causing you a problem they are your responsibility now. Your only defense against them is a relationship with God through his son, Jesus!

I have seen people get angry with God because they do not have the things other people have. Incredibly, God gets blamed for the work of the devil—and his servant demons.

See Forgiveness As a Gift to Yourself

Most of the time, the people we are angry with about a real or imagined slight do not know or care how we feel. The only person who is hurt by an unforgiving spirit is the person who refuses to forgive. This has powerful implications for your mental health. Letting go of grudges, slights, disrespect, and an unnecessarily critical self-assessment will do more to liberate you from the emotional prison that you are in than anything else. You have the key and you can walk out a free person anytime you choose.

I have heard people pray that God will send their children or spouse home. But when God answers and the person shows up after time in jail or prison, they are driven away by relatives who have an unforgiving spirit. Be careful about what you pray for. This underscores the need for the people you have hurt whom you hope to be reunited with when you serve your time, to thoroughly examine themselves, work through their issues, and forgive you. This may require you to make the first move by working through your issues and asking for forgiveness, and forgiving yourself.

Regardless of what was done to you, forgiving and letting the offense go will do you more good than anyone else. Sometimes the hardest person to forgive is yourself because of the depth of your guilt and shame. But by the grace of God and the power of the Holy Spirit it can be done. God forgives. Who are you to have higher standards than God?

Live One Day At A Time

A person is sentenced to jail or prison for a specific period of time. Regardless of how many years the sentence may be, it can only be served one day at a time. No one lives his or her life any other way, whether in or out of prison. Trying to serve a sentence a month or a year at a time will make the slowness of the passage of time unbearable, like looking forward to Christmas when you were a child. Instead of living life one day at a time, children who looked forward to Christmas by thinking in terms of twelve months found that it seemed as if it would never come.

When I get up to walk in the morning, if I think about the two mile end point, I get discouraged about tackling my course. But when I break it up into small increments it seems a whole lot easier to do. Thinking about it, in terms of one quarter of a mile, one half, three fourths, and then a mile, make walking a mile a whole lot easier. Yet, each point brings me closer to my goal of two miles. Our fathers knew this when they sang:

"We are climbing Jacob's Ladder…Every round takes us higher and higher."

They reached their goal one round at a time. The poet understood it who said "It's a cinch by the inch."

Exercise Good Judgment By Understanding The Difference between Street Smart and Spirit Smart

What gets people into trouble is their failure to use good judgment either in their associates or their conduct. Staying out of trouble is the result of exercising good judgment. But more often than not, these persons get into trouble because they either cannot or will not think for themselves. These persons are gullible enough to let others do their thinking. Until they "wise up," they will always be in and out of prison because there is no shortage of people who are willing to use them in criminal activities. Sometimes the persons who fail to use good judgment are the leaders of criminal activities instead of mindless followers. In either case, the consequences are the same—jail or prison. I do not know how many times I have heard lawyers tell judges preparing to sentence their client that they got into trouble because they "got with the wrong crowd." That is another way of saying the person did not use good judgment.

Good judgment is not something that one human being can give another. The Bible teaches us that it comes from God. In the book of James we are told that if any man lacks wisdom he should ask God for it (James 5 NKJV). That, of course, presupposes that the person without wisdom has sense enough to realize it and willingness to seek it from its source. Too many are street smart, but never get spirit smart. People who are street smart are smart enough to commit criminal acts, to survive on the streets through criminal activity, but not smart enough to keep from getting caught. On the other hand, spirit smart persons are smart enough to stay out of trouble and figure out when someone is trying to "put them in a trick," and are able to not only say no to others, but also themselves. This is a compelling reason to get your spiritual house in order as soon as possible.

The book of Proverbs in the Bible is a great collection of wise sayings that speak directly to the predicaments that young men often face. Reading it will do you a lot of good. Proverbs advises young people, among other things, to get wisdom and understanding by listening to the instruction of fathers. But if one's father is absent or does not have the wisdom this task requires, he or she may have to seek it through a reliable surrogate father figure, or as James advises, directly from God, who gives us his word to make us wise (II Tim. 3:15 NKJV). Getting wisdom straight from God is the most direct way to get it, and, regrettably, for all too many, it is the only way because of absent or unwise fathers.

Thankfully, our heavenly Father is always present in the person of the Holy Spirit who is our teacher and guide. With Him you are a whole lot smarter than you will ever be by listening to your buddies or depending on yourself.

2.2 BELIEFS

Get a New World View

The complaint of many persons behind bars is that society does not understand where they are coming from. Unfortunately, in too many instances neither do they. One thing is certain, and that is unless a person changes where he or she is coming from, he or she will end up where he or she has been, jail—or worse, dead!

There is no transformation without a change in one's thinking. This is what I mean by world view. It involves belief, values, and culture. Behavior follows beliefs. How we think is influenced by unarticulated assumptions and beliefs that are part of a person's philosophy of life that are summed up in the word *weltanschauung* or world view.

Although hanging out with the wrong crowd is not a good idea, what gets people in trouble quicker than anything else is not their associates, but their beliefs and thoughts. You do not have any control over others, but you can control what you believe and think. This is the quickest route to becoming a new and better you! As your body was guarded in prison or jail, you must learn to guard your mind if you are going to become a new person and stay out of trouble. Only by changing your thoughts and beliefs can you change the way you behave. As King Solomon put it centuries ago, "As a person thinks so is he" (Proverbs 23:7).

Clarify Your Life Purpose

All of us were put here for some purpose other than to occupy a jail or prison cell and create problems for other people to solve. What is yours? Until you find your purpose in life you will continue to flounder and squander your time and talent. If you are not sure about why you are here and what you are supposed to be doing, I suggest that you read *The Purpose Driven Life* by Rick Warren.[20] As God has equipped you with what you need to be successful in some area of life and to make a contribution to society through the talents and natural gifts you were given, reflection on this subject is a good place to begin. But if it is still not clear, ask God! To be all that you can be requires that you build your life around the purpose you were born to achieve.

2.3 VALUES

Choose a New Set of Values

Do not think values are relative. There are absolute values by which we all should live. They are discovered in the mind through reason. This is called natural law. Some things are wrong, and we know it even without the benefit of formal instruction. We know right from wrong! But the highest and best source of moral instruction is the word of God—the Bible for Christians, the Torah for Jews, The Koran for Muslims and other sacred texts for other faith traditions.

Tell the Truth

The values of the street might have temporarily worked for you or somebody you know. Some of the people you know might still be flying high. Eventually they will be where you are now because the values of the street did not work for you. And guess what? They will not work for you when you get back on the streets. Nowhere is the need for a change in values more clear than in your relationship with those in authority. One of the most respected tenets of street culture is "stop snitching."[21] That is far more than a slogan. In street culture, it expresses antipathy for and distrust of law enforcement by discouragement of cooperation with policemen and prosecutors. It is also part of an unwritten code of silence in the law enforcement community. Wrong is wrong regardless who is doing it. In either case, it allows wrong doers to get away with criminal conduct through a not-so-subtle form of witness intimidation, which frustrates the legitimate goal of law enforcement agencies to protect law abiding citizens—your mother, sister, wife, children, siblings, and other innocents.

What is true of street culture is also true of prison life in the matter of cooperation with guards. The "convict code" prohibits "ratting" on pain of severe bodily injury or death. If you choose to live by the law of the jungle, do not be surprised if you and people you care about are eventually destroyed by it.

One of the best indicators of your rehabilitation is respect for authority and the rule of law. When you come to this place in your life, you recognize that you cannot take the law into your own hands by trying to "right wrongs yourself" as an expression of your manhood. Further, as a citizen, you realize that you have the same obligation to cooperate with the police that everyone else has in the interest of creating a safe community. If you choose to testify in a court of law, the integrity of the system depends upon you telling the truth. How would you like it if your freedom depended on the testimony of someone with a motive to lie?

The worst part of what happens when reliance is too great on the testimony of unreformed and unrepentant criminals is that many innocent people suffer. According to one study, 51 of the 111 wrongful death penalty convictions since the 1970s were based in part on the testimony of witnesses who had a strong motive to lie. This problem is exacerbated by the fact that "one of every four black men from 20 to 29 is behind bars, on probation or on parole."[22] The question is not whether one should cooperate with legal authorities in cleaning up our neighborhoods, but rather whether the word of people facing a stiff sentence can be trusted without a lot of corroboration. In a sense, the question is not whether to "snitch" or not, but whether to tell the truth if you have information concerning the commission of a crime. This is not just a law enforcement issue, but a matter of character. If a person has bad character and believes he can get a reduced sentence by lying on someone else, what do you think he is going to do, laws against false swearing and perjury notwithstanding? If you lie, however, your deception will be discovered as it was in the case of those who were wrongfully sentenced to die for crimes they did not commit—and you will be an even bigger pariah. While you cannot afford to mindlessly go along with those who say you should never cooperate with law enforcement officials, it is hard to understand how much credibility can be given to the word of people who have been liars, cheats, and con men all their lives when deciding someone's guilt or innocence—or life or death. Since in a prison environment, truth is not valued except among fellow inmates, it is considered acceptable to lie to "the man." That is why character is always relevant during cross examination of witnesses and why people will look at what you say with a jaundiced eye for a long time after your release from prison. Too many people live by the credo that "a lying tongue is an abomination in the sight of almighty God, but it is a mighty present help in the time of trouble!"

Biologists describe cooperation as "what happens when someone or something gets a benefit because someone or something else pays a cost." The difficulty of getting people who are in competition for the same benefit to cooperate with each other for their common good, is illustrated by a conundrum known as "the prisoner's dilemma."[23] It involves two prisoners who are separately offered the same plea bargain: If one of them testifies and the other does not, the one who testifies will go free and the one who does not will go to jail for ten years. If both refuse to testify, the prosecutor will only be able to incarcerate them for six months. If each prisoner "rats out" his co-defendant, they both get five-year sentences. Since one does not know what the other prisoner will do, what should each one do? While what you face is not a game, the "prisoner's dilemma" illustrates the moral difficulty people in your predicament resolve with little or no guidance.

Once apprehended, the opportunity for communication or collaboration is either impossible by the terms of bail or because of separation in jail. As was recently seen in the high profile Michael Vick case and many lesser cases, the attitude of a person in trouble is "every man for himself and God for us all." When one's freedom is at stake, the solidarity that made one a brother or partner in crime quickly disappears. Although this illustration addresses cooperation in general, it convincingly shows that the people you thought were your friends will sell you out in a nano-second to save their own skin. It also illustrates the preeminence of cooperation as a strategy for not only individuals, but also communities.

2.4 GOALS

Be Realistic in Setting Goals

I know a young man whose only goal in life was to become a professional or college level basketball coach. The problem was that he was unwilling to start at junior high school, junior varsity, or high school to get the experience necessary to get into college coaching which might then give him a realistic hope of landing a professional job as an assistant coach. But no—for him it was college, pro, or nothing. There are many young athletes who are just as unrealistic about playing college or professional sports.

This pattern is reflected in the lives of many who do not set realistic goals. They beat their heads against a brick wall rather than seek another way to the other side. How many times have we seen this in young people who waste their time thinking they will be a star athlete because they excelled on the playground or on the sand lot? At some point one has to do what is within his or her reach. Continuing to put forth effort in something which you are not suited for leads only to frustration, disappointment, and failure. The answer may be as simple as redirecting your energies and focus to something else. As Arnold and Clifford Lazarus say, "a "switcher" is not the same as a quitter."[24]

Some of the goals you set for yourself before your conviction are no longer available to you because of the fitness requirement that you are irrebuttably presumed to be incapable of meeting by the law. Those include law, medicine, secondary education, and many others.

In modifying your goals, do not go beneath what you are capable of doing. Find another way to put your talents to use in a field that may not have the same requirements. It may mean having to look at vocational education. Successful plasterers, electricians, plumbers, and carpenters often make more money than doctors and lawyers. But their jobs require hard toil.

You cannot get anywhere without a goal. As someone said, "If you do not know where you are going, any road you take will get you there." Goals give our lives direction. If the goal you have been pursuing is unattainable, get another one.

Master The Art of Setting Goals

There are all kinds of goals. For example, there are personal, family, educational, health, financial, vocational, and spiritual goals. Almost any area of life is capable of being assessed in terms of specific things we want to accomplish. It is an excellent way to measure our performance and keep ourselves motivated. But what is important is that the goals are realistic. What is realistic for a person with a record is not the same as what it is for someone without one. Jobs and professions you may have the intellect to handle are off limits if you cannot meet a character or fitness requirement. This means that you may need to reassess what you can do with your life, vocationally. But, there is no reason why you cannot set goals and work towards them in all other areas of life.

What is probably more important than the nature of your goal is whether it is short term or long term. Some things you have to be willing to work for over an extended period of time. These require patience and perseverance in the face of failure and rejection. Perhaps that is what Charles C. Noble meant when he said, "You must have long range goals to keep you from being frustrated by short range failures." That is why most people agree that a goal, especially a long range goal, has to be sufficiently big to keep you challenged and committed to working for its attainment. A small goal that requires too little of you is not likely to keep you motivated.

Many of you have been assaulted on the streets and in prison. Some of you were abused as children. This may explain some of the problems you have in dealing with the issues of daily living. This involves what neuropsychologists call inadequate "Executive Functioning," which could conceivably be the result of an impairment in cognitive functioning as a result of trauma. If you are experiencing an unusually high level of difficulty in setting goals, making plans to achieve your goals, and following through with the plans you have made, you or someone who is trying to help you may want to get an evaluation to make sure there is no physiological or psychological reason for these conditions.

There is medical evidence from head injuries in soldiers and professional football players, which may also explain bad behavior in some people and inability to have normal relationships with others. Consequently, if you have had a history of a head injury, it might be advisable to get an evaluation in order to obtain the help you need to maximize your chance of succeeding outside of prison in performing daily living skills. There are experts in neuropsychology who believe that much of the bad behavior and poor judgment that we see in some people can be related not only to trauma, but also a lack of maturation.

Get to The Right Destination

Stephen R. Covey says one of the habits of people who are "highly effective" is that they "begin with the end in mind."[25] What he means is that they "start with a clear understanding of where they are going." One of the things he suggests to get clarity of direction is a "personal mission statement." It is analogous to a road map. In planning a trip, one has to first know where he or she wants to go. I see so many people whose lives have not amounted to much. What they all have in common is aimlessness. For many it begins in their youth through the inability to decide something as simple as what they want to be. I cannot tell you the number of children who respond to the question, "What do you want to be?" with the answer, "I don't know." It gets worse when grown men and women have not figured out what they want to do with their lives. Yet many of them are in a hurry. The tragedy is that they do not have a clue as to where they are going. Like lemmings, they mindlessly follow the crowd over life's cliffs to their physical or civil death.

To succeed in life, one has to have goals or direction. For some of you, this means redirecting or refocusing your life. No one can do that for you. You have to decide that the road you have been on is carrying you in the wrong direction, stop, and turn around. On the road of life, U-turns are always possible as long as you are in control of the mode of transportation. If you are along with the crowd for the ride, you have to go with whoever is driving,—unless you risk life and limb by jumping out of the vehicle if the driver will not stop because you have decided that you would rather walk backward in the right direction than ride forward the wrong way.

All of us are going somewhere. It may not look like it, but all of us have a destination. It is one we have chosen or one someone chose for us. When I first saw Grand Central Station in New York, I thought that was the most chaotic place I had ever seen. There were thousands of people headed to work through this massive transit system and all of them seemed to know exactly where they were going—except me. If I had not stayed close to the person I was with, I would have never made it through that confusing maze and mass of humanity. We were together on where we were going, but only my guide knew how to get to our destination.

The question is, where are you going? What is your destination? How will you get there? If you have no goals you will never get anywhere. All you will do is go around and around, and where you stop neither you nor anyone else will ever know. But it is likely to be far away from a good place.

Getting some place in life requires that you first have an intended destination because as Henry Kissinger was quoted as saying, "If you don't know where you are going, any road will get you nowhere."[26] Yogi Berra is credited with a humorous variation on this observation: "If you don't know where you are going, you may end up some place else."[27]

Since a "goal is just a destination that you are trying to reach," as Ned Gedman[28] puts it, it is up to you to decide how to reach it. Most of us need a map to plan our travel. What is your plan? One cannot achieve anything worthwhile on a consistent basis without having a definite goal and a plan to make it happen.

Benjamin Mays, the former President of Morehouse College, once said:

> It must be borne in mind…that the tragedy in life does not lie in not reaching your goal. The tragedy lies in having no goal to reach. It isn't a calamity to die with dreams unfulfilled, but it is a calamity not to dream…It is not a disgrace not to reach the stars, but it is a disgrace to have no stars to reach for. Not failure, but low aim is sin.[29]

Aimlessness that begins in school carries over into life as an adult and leads inevitably to a less than satisfactory life. It causes the vast potential with which you were endowed to remain undeveloped.

No realistic goal, regardless of its size, can be reached without consistent and committed effort. Whether a goal is realistic depends upon your personal limitations and those that are imposed by law. Without a criminal record the stars might have been the limit, but now you may have to settle for the sky.

Play Catch-Up

In many sports, when a team is behind, it is usually impossible to make up the deficit in a short period of time or with one play. The best strategy is to "chip away" at the lead by making up a little of the deficit along until the lead is in striking distance. If too much energy is expended to make up the short fall too quickly, the task may prove too exhausting to ever accomplish. Having the persistence to keep at it is the key to ultimately overtaking one's opponent. That is true of personal deficits as well.

Realize That You Don't Have To Hit a Home Run

In baseball there are few players who can consistently hit the ball out of the park. Those who swing for the fences at every bat are sure to strike out a lot. The idea is to score. One cannot make it to home plate if he never gets on base. It has been said by many commentators, but it is still true that you cannot "steal" first base. That is the beginning point. Everybody starts out at the same place—home plate. But not everyone has what it takes to get on base and make it back to home plate. Regardless of whether a baseball player hits a single or a home run, "it is still necessary to run the bases. Sometimes players hurt their teams by trying to make up large deficits with one swing of the bat. As that is not always possible in baseball, you cannot expect to do that in getting back into the swing of things on the outside.

The teams that seem to win with the most consistency are those which know how to manufacture a run through "small ball." That involves station to station base-running. The hitter gets on base and moves around the bases, one base at a time, until he eventually gets home. This is far more like the way life is lived than hitting a home run. The mind set that gets people focused on a "big score" is behind the temptation to turn to crime instead of working at an honest job and saving for one's wants and needs.

Turn Pro in Something Worthwhile

One of the worst things young people do is waste time on things that do not amount to a "hill of beans." Ask many of our youth what they plan to do with their lives, and they will tell you they want to be a professional athlete. Ask them who their heroes and heroines are, and they will list sports stars. The NCAA has an ad that tries to dispel the myth that anyone can easily make it into professional sports and celebrates the accomplishments of athletes who found success in other fields. Its message features young people who did something other than professional sports because they got an education. The punch line was that they were "turning pro in something other than sports." That is the reality for the overwhelming majority of high school and college athletes.

Even the small number who "turn pro" because they have the athletic prowess to compete at the highest level of their game often fall woefully short because they have not developed character traits to succeed in sports or life. "Turning pro" in anything requires, at a minimum, the ability to regulate one's conduct. In fact, it is the privilege of self-regulation that distinguishes a professional from a member of a trade. In sports, the expectations are entirely different at the professional level than anywhere else. Going to bed on time, eating right, staying out of trouble and staying in shape are the professional athlete's responsibility—not the coach's. This is true in every other area in which a person "turns pro." It is the employee's responsibility, for example, to acquire the skills that are necessary to get the job done and show up every day ready, willing, and able to flawlessly execute the moves that make-up his or her life's work.

CHAPTER THREE
Becoming the Person You Were Meant To Be

Many people look back on their lives with regret. They are the people who say "I wish I had, I could have, I would have, or should have." Their attitude is summed up in the phrase: "coulda, shoulda, woulda." In ability, they have everything they need to succeed, but they never achieve what they are capable of.

It is not enough to talk about potential. Someone said all potential means is that you have not done what you were capable of yet. At some point one has to "just do it."

All of us start out with the potential to become whatever our maker had in mind for us. The secret to success in life is not only discovering our purpose and living in accordance with it, but also refusing to allow bad habits or broken character to keep us from becoming all we were meant to be. This is the issue that is explored in this chapter.

3.1 HABITS

Break Bad Habits

Most of us associate the word habit with negative, self-defeating behavior like washing our hands before eating or brushing our teeth. We may think we developed our habits on our own. But that is far from the truth. Manufacturers of everything from aspirin to watches have learned how to manipulate the habits of consumers to make large sums of money.[1] If you are going to succeed in staying out of trouble, you have to learn the cues that trigger your behavior or habits. There are bad habits, to be sure. But there are also good habits. Usually, good habits must compete with and overcome bad habits. The longer the bad habit has been practiced, the harder it is to break. Consequently, it is better to avoid bad habits than try to break them or replace them with good habits. Who you ultimately become is the result of the habits you form as the "Five Watches" of an anonymous poet remind us:

"Watch your thoughts; they become words.
Watch your words, they become actions.
Watch your actions; they become habits.
Watch your habits; they become character.
Watch your character; it becomes your destiny."[2]

Ultimately, the key to becoming the best person you can be is an honest examination of your habits. If you spend as much time working on this area of your life, your mind, and spirit as you do body building, for example, there is no telling what you will become. It is a matter of priorities, where you get the biggest "bang for your buck," and "keeping the main thing the main thing." I realize that some may associate body building with issues of self-esteem and survival out of a feeling that "only the strong survive." If one is a giant physically, but a ninety- pound weakling mentally, morally, and spiritually, what does it profit him? Read the sports pages of any newspaper, and you will see accounts of the wreckage of once promising lives that were ruined by things that did not profit them anything. The athletes had it all – but they did not have a moral compass that was able to keep them going in the right direction because their lives were dominated by bad habits.

For most of us, the biggest challenge is changing bad habits that have been reinforced by years of practice – and success in using them to get what we want. The habits which work on the streets, in a gang, or in a criminal enterprise are incompatible with the requirements of "conventional society." They are of limited value in the real world which recognizes and rewards habits such as work, punctuality, respect for authority, and honesty. That is why Ghandi considered "wealth without work" to be a social sin.

If you habitually lie, steal, or con to get what you want, do not expect change in your modus operandi to occur overnight. For some of you, it may take several incarcerations to realize the futility of your old way of behaving. At that point you may at least be willing to look at habit-replacement. But if you are as smart as you think you are, why is that necessary? Once is one time too many!

The temptation will be strong to take short-cuts. But you must have the discipline to say no to yourself and practice the good habits that you are forming like staying at home at night, going to bed at a reasonable hour, and working for what you want instead of begging or running scams on gullible people. Whatever you do long enough will become a habit – that is true of good things as well as bad things. Which one you do reveals the true nature of your character because it is shown more clearly by what you do than what you say.

Develop The Ten Habits of Successfully Rehabilitated Ex-Inmates

With apologies to Stephen Covey, let me give you my list of habits that distinguish a successfully rehabilitated person from one who is caught in the revolving door of the prison to which he or she was sentenced. A successfully rehabilitated person:

Obeys the law and follows all rules and conditions of probation or parole – no exceptions or excuses (including special conditions because of the nature of the crime);
Accepts responsibility for himself or herself;
Sets realistic goals and develops a plan to accomplish them;
Works for what he or she wants and pays his or her bills;

Gets and stays drug free and does not abuse alcohol;

Marries and supports his or her children;

Deals with mental health issues, if any;

Watches the people with whom he or she associates;

Gets right with God and gets in a good church where he or she can grow into all God intended for him or her to become (for some it may be a mosque or other institutions) and;

Gets his or her civil rights restored, participates in the political life of his or her community, and accepts the responsibility involved in citizenship.

These habits, based upon my observations, are found in people who succeed in overcoming their criminal record. But they are especially important for a person who is committed to staying out of trouble. If nothing else, this list will give you a yard stick with which to measure your progress.

3.2 CHARACTER

Work On Your Character, and Your Reputation Will Improve Too

There is a difference between one's character and one's reputation. As many have observed, reputation is what people think you are and character is what you really are when no one else is looking. You cannot do a lot about what people think about you. But because character is the result of choices that are made, you can change it because of the ability to make different choices. Your mind is under your control.

A lot of people will not look beyond your prison record. For them, that is who you are. That is your reputation and "once a con always a con," they say. I have heard character witnesses tell courts the person on trial or being sentenced "was acting out of character." That is hard to believe because on the minds of many people character is who you are all the time, even in unguarded moments.

If you work to rebuild your character by changing the way you think and making better choices, eventually you will develop a better reputation. I agree with Thomas Paine's observation, however, that "character is much easier kept than recovered."[3]

What you have been through represents moral and spiritual failure. Your failure has huge financial and social consequences. What you did has not just affected you, but also your spouse, children, parents, siblings, friends, taxpayers – and whatever church you held membership in. We are so connected that whatever happens to any of us affects us all. It is like casting a stone into a pond. Whatever we do has a ripple effect. You owe a lot of people an apology – because you have hurt and disappointed a lot of people who believed in you. The first step on the road to rebuilding your re-lationships is to accept responsibility for what you have done. Do not blame anybody else. Apologize, and make amends to those you have hurt, to the best of your ability. But care needs to be taken in how you do it. There may be a court order that forbids you to have no contact with the victim. If you assaulted or raped somebody, you are the last person the victim ever wants to see again. The perception of a threat will be created just by your presence, and that could land you back in jail. The desire for vengeance may still be strong in the person or his or her family, and that could result in your bodily harm. That may be true of folk you robbed or stole from. Making amends in this case may need to be through a trusted intermediary such as a pastor or parole officer. The same may also be true of apologizing. If you are familiar with the teachings of Alcoholics Anonymous, you know that there is an emphasis on making amends to those you have hurt. While that is ordinarily a good idea, you can not do it without possibly running a serious risk of violating a condition of your parole.

But there is not likely to be any real healing for you or your victim without in some way coming to terms with it. Keep in mind that you have no control over anybody but yourself. You may not have any choice but to wait for the victim to make the first move.

People in business are accustomed to using what belongs to others and paying for it. When they borrow money, for example, the interest they pay is little more than rent on its use. In the same sense, that concept applies to vacation property, cars, or anything else for which a better use can be found for their money – if they have any.

Not only is other folk's money used, but also their minds. That happens every time professional services are obtained. Doctors, lawyers, accountants, and many other professionals are happy to lend their minds – and expertise, for a price.

If other people's money and minds are available for a price, there is no reason other things such as their good name can not also be borrowed. This happens every time trial lawyers agree to represent a person who is accused of a criminal offense. In wrapping his or her arms around this person and standing between him or her and the awesome power of the state, the defense lawyer puts his own name on the line. The lawyer's competence, credibility and character were bought. In a sense, the client has to be as discerning in his or her choice of a lawyer as lawyers are in selecting clients. The client has, by retaining a lawyer, borrowed the use of his or her name – character and reputation for the duration of the representation. At least for that time, the identification of the lawyer with his or her client could give him or her, the benefit of the lawyer's good name.

A person coming out of prison obviously does not have a good name in the eyes of society. If he or she cannot get what is needed to get on with life because of a bad name, there is no reason – under the right circumstances – he or she cannot legally and morally use someone else's. The last thing a person coming out of prison needs is more legal trouble. Do not misunderstand what I am saying. Identity theft is not an option. Your continued liberty depends upon avoiding further criminal conduct. What I have in mind is what happens every time a letter of recommendation is submitted or permission is granted to use someone's name as a reference. Never use someone's name as a reference without permission. The person who writes a letter or serves as a reference puts his or her name behind yours. Assuming that the person has a good reputation, what he or she says about you can make all the difference with a prospective employer in the same way the lawyer's good name helps persuade a jury.

Whether you can use someone else's name depends upon the relationship you have with him or her and whether you have his or her permission. That is likely to be influenced by such things as your willingness to work hard, devotion to your family, church attendance, evidence of rehabilitation, and acceptance of responsibility for the situation that led to your incarceration.

The only place I know of where you can get a pass because of your criminal record is the U. S. Army, which has a long history of providing opportunities to non-white people that are not available in the larger society. It is not just about being gracious. The conflicts that this nation is in around the world have stretched our military resources almost to the breaking point. Reaching recruiting goals for an all volunteer army is increasingly difficult as casualties mount. To help meet its needs, the Army has been granting an increasingly large number of waivers to recruits with criminal backgrounds. They are called "moral waivers" and are issued for serious offenses such as aggravated assault, burglary, robbery, and vehicular homicide. The military claims to automatically exclude drug traffickers, and sexually violent offenders.[4]

At the same time this kind of grace was being offered, the criminal behavior of some of the new recruits continued to show up. For example, in 2006 the Pentagon reported that sexual assaults in the military increased by 24 percent.[5] There are other reports of gratuitous violence directed at fellow soldiers and detainees.

What does this mean to you? The military may still be an option for some of you. But if you do not change your character, your criminal career may continue even while on military duty, and this will result in harsher treatment than you would get in the civilian criminal justice system. There are many who will rightly ask whether the security of this nation should be entrusted to people who through "moral waivers" have not shown that they can be trusted to do what is right and control themselves. While there is something to be said for giving a person a second chance, the problem is that in the absence of evidence that his or her character issue has been fixed, there are many people who do not think giving a person with bad character a gun and a uniform is a good idea.

Repair Your Character

The time to start down the road towards character repair and rehabilitation is not when you get out of jail or prison, but the moment you are convicted. An attitude of contrition and acceptance of responsibility may result in a reduced sentence. Protestations of innocence in the face of overwhelming evidence of guilt may get the book thrown at you.

Once inside, become a model prisoner. Stay away from gangs. Mind your own business. Use your time well. Many people have come out of jail better, not bitter because they used their time to read or even earn a college degree. The life of Malcolm X provides a case in point. He became a voracious reader and that served him well in his life's work.[6]

Becoming a career criminal has more down side risks and consequences than it is worth. The disincentives to crime have never been greater. More and more states are getting tough with criminals. What is more, a long sentence means what it says because some refuse to let people off for good behavior. In some instances state prosecutors are deferring to the federal government, and in the federal system, a sentence is far more likely to be long and served than in the state system.

Another disincentive is that being a criminal has never been more hazardous to your health. Some states have passed laws that allow homeowners to shoot first and ask questions later. They do not have to retreat. If you are caught in their house they can now shoot you with impunity.

The late Lester Maddox, a former segregationist governor of Georgia, once said, "What this state needs is a better class of prisoners."[7] This is oxymoronic because if the people who end up in prison were of a "better class" they probably would not have ended up in prison in the first place. The class of prisoners is improved when we as a society deal with and overcome:

Family disintegration and dysfunction
Childhood abuse and neglect
Spiritual poverty
Educational failure
Unemployment
Lack of job skills
Illiteracy
Drug dependency and alcoholism
Bad character
Mental illness
Bad parenting
Out of wedlock pregnancy

The quip of Governor Maddox is reminiscent of the Starkist Tuna commercial which tells us that the company wants tuna that "tastes good instead of tuna with good taste." This goes to the heart of the distinction between character and reputation. It is what we really are that counts – and not what we are on the surface. There are people who believe that "genes are destiny." But what is probably closer to the truth is the maxim that "character is destiny!" It, more than anything else, determines how your life will turn out.

For one to be seen as a person of character usually means, at a minimum, that he does not have a criminal record. Having a prison record cannot be changed. While it may be possible to expunge an arrest that did not result in a prosecution, it is impossible to remove a conviction through this process. The same is also true of a prosecution that does not result in a conviction. Your record will follow you all of your life. Very few people receive pardons or commutations.

I never cease to be amazed by the people I encounter who have thrown away their good name through bad conduct and who seek legal advice on how they can expunge their record. One of my adult friends called to ask for help writing a letter to a judge to get his record "sealed." There are times when arrests that did not result in prosecution can be expunged, but there is no way to change a record of bad conduct. Your record follows you. Even if a charge is expunged, it cannot erase the experience or others' perception of you. But character involves more than just a criminal record. There are many people who have never been in jail who have bad character. But a person with a criminal record is subjected to closer scrutiny when considered for a job or any other benefit that free people take for granted. In a court, the burden of proof is on the state to prove guilt beyond a reasonable doubt. In society, the burden is on you to prove your worth or merit by a standard that is just as hard to meet. Fair- minded people will give you that chance, which is the most you can expect. With that, you can live your past down. Those who are not fair will take the easy way out by refusing to hire people with a record.

Lists of virtue vary depending upon such things as race and class. For example, William J. Bennett's[8] list includes self-discipline, compassion, responsibility, friendship, work, courage, perseverance, honesty, loyalty, and faith. While there is overlap, Steven Barboza's[9] list of African-American values includes self-discipline, courage, honesty, self-esteem, work, tenacity, creativity, faith, family, community, love, friendship, companionship, responsibility, respect, and loyalty. The virtues on either list will serve you well. Too often, young people choose vices instead of virtues and as a result they end up where you are. Many young people never had a chance to succeed in life because of the circumstances of their birth. But even people who are born under bad circumstances can make it if they have at least one parent or a committed mentor who will hold them accountable for practicing and developing virtues.

Only people who are willing to put forth an effort to remake themselves have any real chance to overcome flaws in their character. It is a choice. As it involves choice, no one can do it for another person.

One can choose the person he or she wants to become. No one in his or her right mind sets out to become a career criminal. It happens because of bad choices and failure to prepare for something constructive.

Understand The Difference Between Character and Reputation

"A fresh start" in another community away from the toxic personal and family relationships that contributed to your inability to stay out of trouble may be the quickest way to improve your reputation. The reason is that reputation unlike character is what people think you are. If you do not tell people you are an ex-inmate and do not look or act like one, no one will know. If asked about your past by a prospective employer, you must tell the truth – always, no exceptions. Honesty is the best policy. But if it is not on any application form and does not come up in an interview, no one will ever be able to say you falsified your resume or got a job under false pretenses. Whether you need to tell anyone about your past in this context is up to you – your good judgment. Arguably, it would be far better to be "up -front" about it even when you are not asked because I have seen people lose jobs after they were hired in security conscious industries, especially after 9/11. The same issues come up in romantic relationships. Total transparency is absolutely essential. If you are HIV positive, for example, and do not disclose it to a sexual partner, you can be prosecuted for it. The best and safest policy is to avoid sexual activity outside of heterosexual marriage. This is of great importance because of the incidence of AIDS and HIV in black women, which, is rightly or wrongly, explained in part by sexual contact with people who are coming out of prison who engaged in homosexual acts either voluntarily or through assaults and intravenous drug use. Still, your reputation can not help but benefit from a change of scenery because of the definitions we are using – if you clean up your act and do what is right.

Character is an entirely different matter. Your character follows you wherever you go. Whatever you are in one place is what you are or will be wherever you go. Again, that is why someone said "reputation is what people think you are" but "character is what you are when no one else is looking" at you. This is why D. L. Moody said "Character is what you are in the dark."[10] It comes into play when no authority figure is around to regulate your conduct. Given the nature of character, it cannot be changed by simply moving from one place to another. We saw this with "evacuees" or "refugees" from New Orleans after Hurricane Katrina. Many of the cities where they found refuge were glad to see some of this population leave their communities because of the increase in crime that was associated with their presence.

The hard work of rehabilitation deals with you and involves nothing less than making yourself "fit for yourself to know" and live with. That is why much of this book deals with individual issues of values and choices.

Get A Good Name

One of the prerequisites for success is getting a job, and the mark of a person of character is a good name. If you cannot use your damaged name to get what you want wan, the solution is using someone else's. That is done every time someone agrees to write you a letter of recommendation or serve as a personal reference. That cannot be done unless you give evidence of change.

Set a Good Example

Somebody is watching you. Your example may inspire youthful admirers or lead them astray. There are many young people who think a prison record is "cool." They walk the street wearing their clothes the way they think inmates wear theirs. You see them walking the streets with their britches hanging down because they refuse to wear a belt as if this shameful style is something to be proud of. They do not know that prison guards take belts away from prisoners, and they have no choice about how their clothes fit. If you are not a sex offender, one of the best services you can render when you are rehabilitated and released is to tell young people the consequences of becoming a "gang banger" and criminal. Through this means you can show that redemption and atonement are possible.

People will react to you when they find out that you are an ex-inmate in one of the following ways:

1.	Fear	6.	Distrust
2.	Dis-ease	7.	Suspicion
3.	Avoidance	8.	Resentment
4.	Hate	9.	Contempt
5.	Loathing	10.	Rejection

Why make yourself a target of their loathing by looking and acting like a hoodlum? I once heard a coach say to his team that a player plays the way he looks and practices. If he is sloppy in one area, he is likely to be that way in others, too.

Get Some Glue

In my opinion, the glue that holds a person's life together is Jesus who can do what "all the king's horses and all the kings men" can not do and that is put Humpty Dumpty back together again. In the Bible this is expressed by the word consist. It means "to put together" in Greek. The Apostle Paul used the word in this sense when he wrote of Christ that:

He is before all things
And in him all things
hold together. Col. 1:17 (NKJV).

The worldwide trend towards secularism shows that Christ has been rejected in favor of purveyors of humanistic world views. It parallels the incredible degree to which people are broken in mind and spirit and provides stark evidence of the fact that they have come "unglued." In order to fix the brokenness that so many suffer from and achieve some semblance of wholeness, we need the glue of Christ's presence. That is the only way Humpty Dumpty and the rest of us can be put back together again when we allow our character to be destroyed.

Don't Try to Game the System

Too many people misuse their intelligence to try to "game the system." The bad thing about that is that it reveals the moral deficit that got them into trouble in the first place. It also shows that it is possible to be too smart for one's own good, and that it is possible to outsmart oneself. An example of this is the attempt by a high profile politician with no record of drug addiction or alcoholism, attempting to reduce the amount of his time in prison by enrolling in a drug rehabilitation program. Although it initially resulted in a reduction in the time he was to serve, when it was publicized, his release date was recalculated and the benefit he received from this ploy was taken from him. For good measure, what was left of his reputation was sullied even further by this attempt to game the system. Everyone who enters a drug or alcohol rehabilitation program is not there to get sober. Some are there to get out of jail or prison as soon as possible.

There are, no doubt, countless other ways that people behind bars with lots of time on their hands attempt to "game the system." Most, if not all of them, are discovered before the person in jail or prison is released. Imagine how something like that will play with a State Parole Board or a potential employer. People who are already wary of hiring ex-inmates will see this conduct as the most recent evidence of the system's inability to reform habitual con artists and crooks. This is one of many reasons that the best policy is to be honest even if it costs you in the short run. It is also why rehabilitation begins a long time before a person is released from prison. What you are doing now is preparing for what you will do when you get out. You have to think about how your behavior will go over with people whose favor you will need to reach your goal in the future.

CHAPTER FOUR
Getting and Keeping Yourself Together

For some people, life is a constant struggle to find themselves. They move one step forward and two steps backward. As old people in the rural community where I grew up used to say, "They are like the bear – making tracks, and getting no where."

The challenge of getting somewhere in life is largely dependent upon getting and keeping ourselves together. That happens when we get grown not just physically, but also mentally. While I am convinced that spiritual growth is absolutely indispensable to a person who is trying to get herself or himself together, the most important work in this process takes place in the mind. The spirit works in this part of a person's life just as he does in every other area. Spirituality and thinking are not mutually exclusive. People who try to live without a relationship with Jesus usually lose everything, including their minds, when their lives unravel. Consequently, the focus of my advice is the inner life.

This chapter is based on my conviction that the conduct that evidences your failure to get and keep yourself together will not change until you get some glue that is strong enough to get the job done.

4.1 MATURITY

Grow Up

Becoming a grown-up is easier said than done. But it is essential. The almighty puts us into relationships, families, and even jails to grow us up. The Apostle Paul said:

> "When I was a child, I spoke as a child, I understood as a child, I thought as a child; but when I became a man, I put away childish things." (I Cor. 13:11 NKJV).

> "And we know that all things work together for good to those who love God, to those who are the called according to His purpose." (Rom. 8:28 NKJV).

Putting away childish things is the object of growth towards maturity.
A lot of people behind bars worry their parents by writing or calling them and

telling them how badly they are being treated by guards or fellow inmates. They have no way of dealing with your personal safety. Although some of you think the "convict code" will protect you, the guards or correctional officers are more likely to perform this function than inmates. Your parents cannot make your lawyer speed up the legal process. Do not try to put your parents on a "guilt trip." Remember, you got yourself in the mess you are in.

Your parents do not owe you anything. Growing up and becoming a man or woman means that you take care of your own business – and pay your own way. If you have to stay at your parent's home until you get on your feet, insist on paying rent, helping with chores, and respecting the rules of the house by not staying out late or engaging in anti-social or criminal conduct there or anywhere else. Do not use your parent's address to get your mail and "shack" somewhere else. That is part of the old irresponsible pattern that got you where you are now. If you are a woman and do not have any children, thank God. All having a "ready made" family will do is reduce your chance of ever getting married. Too few men are responsible enough to marry you and take care of their own children, let alone someone else's children.

Do not think manhood is measured in terms of how many women you have or how many children you produce. Much of the trouble our communities are suffering from now is the result of this fallacious, recidivist thinking. A real man takes care of his responsibilities to his wife and children – and attends to his business by standing on his own feet.

4.2 PURPOSE

Don't Let the Past Mess Up the Present
The key is to let go of the things and relationships from your past that you cannot do anything about any way. The only place the past exists is in your head. Let it go. Concentrate on what you can do something about – the present. The past exerts powerful influence over the present and the future, especially if it is not dealt with through forgiveness, counseling, and spiritual rebirth. Otherwise, the past is always imported into the present and keeps you from ever building a life with a bright future. There are some things you have to let go and stop dragging around with you like a ball and chain on your ankles – or worse, your mind or in your head.

Rehearse Your Life Story
In confronting your criminal history, it is possible to discover things about yourself that are of inestimable value in going forward with your life. The past should not handicap you. Rather, it should help you by allowing you to "look backward for the purpose of living forward."

All of us have a story. That is how we live our lives. The narrative and themes of our life story are ignored at our peril. In coming to terms with yourself and making peace with your past, it is essential to look at the facts of your story and then distill from them the concepts and values that you can learn. If the lessons or experiences were learned, you are far more likely to avoid a recurrence of the behavior on which they are based than if you ignore them.

Regardless of how ugly the facts are, you need to look at them. Not to feel shame, but to keep them from creating a problem for you again.

Don't Throw The Rest of Your Life Away

You have an opportunity to start your life over, with the benefit of far more wisdom than you had when you began. The conventional thinking is that jail has been a place for you to refine your skill as a criminal by learning from like-minded felons. If that happens and you try to apply those lessons in a life of post-incarceration criminal activity, then you will get labeled a predatory psychopath who is incapable of redemption. In a word, that would be as foolish as it is futile. You will end up back in jail.

You were put on this earth for something and that was not to occupy a jail or prison cell. But if you choose to live your life that way, society will spare no expense to make sure that people like you are locked up as long as necessary to protect people from you.

4.3 HOPE

Do Not Feel Helpless or Hopeless

You always have options. They may not be readily apparent, but there is something you can do to change the circumstances of your life. That is why you need counseling from people who can give you good advice. Only in hell is there no hope. In Dante's classic, *The Inferno*, an inscription is written on the entrance to hell which says, "Abandon All Hope, You Who Enter Here."[1] Regardless of how bad the place may be where you are now, it is not hell, unless you allow it to snuff out your hope. If you are still in prison, it is not hell (Hades) because that is the place from which no one returns. Just about everyone eventually returns from prison.

Remember That the Game Is Not Over

Life is like a basketball or football game. It is divided into definable periods. Your experience is analogous to that of a team that has blown leads and finds itself behind after the first half of the game.

As there is no ten-point shot to make up a twenty point deficit or a two touchdown play to overcome a three touchdown lead, there is no easy way to get out of the hole you are in. With good coaching, teams often overcome their poor first half performance and win against great odds. After stinking-up the joint with poor play in the first half of your life, you, too, can snatch victory out of the jaws of defeat if you adjust the way you play the game. You need a good game plan for the second half. Consider what got you behind in the game and make enough adjustments in the way you handle what your opponents throw at you to overcome them.

Get The One Thing You Cannot Live Without

Your survival of incarceration depends as much upon hope as your ability to make it outside the prison. We learned this from letters from people who were in German concentration camps in World War II[2] and from Victor Frankl,[3] the Austrian psychiatrist. The people in those camps who had hope, however slim, survived and those who did not, perished. For them it could have been something as flimsy as a rumor of something good happening. What is it for you? For Christians, "when their back is against the wall, it is faith in Jesus and their belief that the Lord will make a way somehow." It is important to keep a positive outlook and realize that your life is not over. For some, it will mean countless hours in a law library working on "writs" trying to win their freedom. For others it may be looking forward to being reunited with parents, children, spouse, boyfriend or girlfriend. Whatever it is, it is essential to keep hope that life is going to get better. I believe that is what Rev. Jessie Jackson means when he says, "Keep hope alive."

Darnell G. Neister said: "Remove hope from a man and you make him a beast."[4] Why? He has nothing to live for. Hopelessness leads to destructiveness in every area of life. The remedy is a good dose of hope. In fact, Orison Sweet Marden said, "There is no medicine like hope, no incentive so great, and no tonic so powerful as expectation of something better tomorrow."[5] Nothing is as effective as hope in staving off depression and the mental health issues that are so often associated with living under bad circumstances.

Someone observed that it is possible to live up to seventy days without food, ten days without water, and six minutes without air. But it is impossible to live without hope. The truth of this was demonstrated by survivors of Nazi Concentration Camps. Those who "kept hope alive" survived. For some, according to Victor Frankl, it was anticipation of seeing family members again.[6] Other survivors had hope of living to tell their story to the world by bearing witness to German atrocities. Having something to live for makes a big difference in one's ability to survive when bad things happen.

4.4 ATTITUDE

See Opportunity in Adversity

Theodore Roosevelt said: "Do what you can, with what you have, where you are."[7] Booker T. Washington said to "let down your bucket where you are."[8] There are opportunities, if you recognize them, even in prison. Paul the Apostle made converts among his Roman guards even while he was in chains. Many people have written notable books. There were people who made money even during the Depression era. Whether you see opportunities where you are is largely a matter of attitude — and outlook. Someone has said, "The pessimist majors in mistakes, misfortunes, and misery; the optimist accentuates assets, abundance, and advantages." That was the case when Jesus fed five thousand people. Most of the disciples were negative in their assessment of the situation. They could not see any way for it to be done. But one disciple started looking around to see what assets were available and found a little boy with a lunch of five loaves of bread and two fishes. When it was made available to Jesus, it was multiplied to the point that not only was the multitude fed, but there was food left over.

I agree with Chuck Swindoll – "You are in charge of your attitude."[9] Of all the things that you can do to improve your life, you will get more bang for your buck by adjusting your attitude. It may not take much of a change. But it will produce better results than almost any other thing you can do. Perhaps that is why William James, the father of psychology, said: "The greatest discovery of my generation is that human beings can alter their lives by altering their attitude of mind."[10]

Your attitude can be positive or negative. Both are necessary. There are some things that you should be negative about – the conduct that got you in trouble, the friends who exerted bad influence on you, and the neighborhood where you did "your thing." But these should not obscure the positive. It takes both a negative and positive terminal on a battery for it to have power. But, in your outlook on life there is no substitute for a positive attitude. It determines not only what, but whether you see life's opportunities. This point is reflected in the pithy words attributed to Frederick Longbridge, who said: "Two men looked through prison bars – one saw mud, the other stars."[11]

According to Clement Stone, "There is little difference in people; but that little difference makes a big difference. The little difference is attitude. The big difference is whether it is positive or negative."[12]

Attitude is so important that some business men evaluate applicants for jobs by giving "five points for availability, five points for adaptability, five points for ability, and eighty-five points to attitude." It is difficult to argue with Lou Holtz's observation:

"Ability is what you are capable of doing.
Motivation determines what you do.
Attitude determines how well you do it."[13]

Look On the Bright Side

Many people have been through what you have experienced and went on to have a successful life. Some of the best examples are as follows:

1. Paul the Apostle
2. Mahatma Gandhi
3. O Henry
4. Martin Luther King, Jr.
5. Nelson Mandela
6. Malcolm X
7. Charles Colson
8. Nathan McCall
9. Joseph
10. Jeremiah
11. Alexander Solzhenitzyn
12. Dietrich Bonhoeffer
13. Nehru

14. Peter the Apostle
15. John Bunyan
16. Socrates
17. Martin Luther
18. Sir Walter Raleigh

Many of them did their most productive work while they were in jail or prison, or after their release. While time in jail or prison is nothing to be proud of, it does not have to be the end of the world. Whether it is a good or bad experience depends on how you see it. If it makes you a better person and you use it to the best possible advantage, it could be transformed from a negative experience to one of the best things that ever happened to you – especially if you learn something from it that sets you on the right course!

Hang in There

This is another way of talking about perseverance, tenacity, and persistence. It is stickability, determination, and willingness to hang in there in the face of great difficulty. Without this essential character trait, many of the good things in life will never be obtained. Anything worth having is almost always difficult to get. That is true of education, vocational training, and a good job. With these things and most other things in life there is "no easy way out."

People who have this quality are difficult to discourage, defeat, or keep down. You are going to be told "no" a whole lot more times than you will receive a positive response. This quality will keep you knocking on doors after you have been turned down for jobs. It will keep you from giving up. That is the quality of a good salesman or a good baseball player. Having a high tolerance for rejection is what I am talking about. Baseball is, as someone put it, a game of failure. In no other game and no other place in life can you fail seven times out of ten and be considered successful.

Do you keep fighting when the going gets tough or do you throw in the towel and say as Roberto Duran said in his fight with Sugar Ray Leonard, "No more, No more?"[4] Life is a struggle for everyone, regardless of his or her criminal record. The ability to hang in there is necessary for all of us.

When I was a child I used to hear people say, "When the going gets tough the tough get going." It is perhaps more accurate to say the tough keep going in spite of their circumstances. That is how some define courage, which is another essential quality.

There are people who have grown so discouraged by their inability to get a job that they give up – and stop looking. These are the people who live on the edge of society and in their desperation resort to crime to "survive." Think what their lives would be like if they applied the same talent for surviving on the streets to something constructive, instead of giving up on making it the right way like everybody else – hanging in there.

Change Your Vocabulary

Make sure the word "no" stays in your vocabulary. The ability to say "no" to yourself and to temptation will make all the difference in your ability to stay out of trouble. It is the essence of self-discipline.

When I was a young man, people used to say, "If you make your bed hard you will have to lie in it." Too often people are faced with difficult circumstances that are of their own making. They tell themselves, "I can't do this." You may be saying that, but it can be done and you can do it – if you want to do it!

They used to say, "Quitters never win and winners never quit." Life is a continuing struggle. The attitude you have to keep is reflected in the words of the anonymous poet who wrote:

> When things go wrong, as they sometimes will,
> When the road you're trudging seems all uphill,
> When the funds are low and the debts are high
> And you want to smile, but you have to sigh,
> When care is pressing you down a bit,
> Rest! if you must – but never quit.
> Life is queer, with its twists and turns,
> As every one of us sometimes learns,
> And many a failure turns about
> When he might have won if he'd stuck it out;
> Stick to your task, though the pace seems slow –
> You may succeed with one more blow.
> Success is failure turned inside out –
> The silver tint of the clouds of doubt –
> And you never can tell how close you are,
> It may be near when it seems afar;
> So stick to the fight when you're hardest hit –
> It's when things seem worst that YOU MUSTN'T QUIT.[15]

Another word you need to get out of your vocabulary is "can't." The poet who wrote "Can't" said it far better than I can when he wrote:

> Can't is the worst word that's written or spoken;
> Doing more harm here than slander and lies;
> On it is many a strong spirit broken,
> And with it many a good purpose dies.
> It springs from the lips of the thoughtless each morning
> And robs us of courage we need through the day:
> It rings in our ears like a timely sent warning
> And laughs when we falter and fall by the way.
>
> Can't is the father of feeble endeavor,
> The parent of terror and halfhearted work;

It weakens the efforts of artisans clever,
And makes of the toiler an indolent shirk.
It poisons the soul of the man with a vision,
It stifles in infancy many a plan;
It greets honest toiling with open derision
And mocks at the hopes and the dreams of a man.

Can't is a word none should speak without blushing;
To utter it should be a symbol of shame;
 Ambition and courage it daily is crushing;
It blights a man's purpose and shortens his aim.
Despise it with all of your hatred of error;
Refuse it the lodgment it seeks in your brain;
Arm against it as a creature of terror,
And all that you dream of you someday shall gain.

Can't is the word that is foe to ambition,
An enemy ambushed to shatter your will;
Its prey is forever the man with a mission
And bows but to courage and patience and skill.
Hate it, with hatred that's deep and undying,
For once it is welcomed 'twill break any man;
Whatever the goal you are seeking, keep trying
And answer this demon by saying, "I can."[16]

The word 'can't', when translated, often means won't.

If a person in your predicament does not want to change or give up bad habits, it is more often a matter of not wanting to do something than inability to do it! You will be amazed at what you will accomplish when you want to do something instead of telling yourself you cannot do it.

Avoid A Bad Attitude

With good reason, any time someone of another race says a black man has a bad attitude, it usually causes him to recoil. That may be equally true of other non-white people. But that does not make one's attitude any less important. It is easier to deal with someone who is humble instead of arrogant. While you do not have to grovel or surrender your manhood or dignity, it is necessary to remember that "pride goes before destruction." (Proverbs 16:18 NKJV).

Nobody owes you anything. You are not entitled to special treatment. The quickest way to get on the bad side of the folk you need to help you get back on track is to act as if you are "God's gift" and that they ought to thank you for the privilege of helping you.

It is true that "your attitude determines altitude"– how high you go. It also determines longitude – how far you go.

Folk who say thank you when someone does them a favor are likely to get a better reception every time than the person who takes people for granted. That is as true of friends and relatives as it is employers. Your behavior dictates who you are, not what others think or say.

Try A Little Humble Pie

Some of worst bragging occurs in prison by people who do not have anything to brag about. All bragging does is show others how you feel about yourself. It is seen as an attempt to compensate for low self-esteem.

It is hard for some people to be humble under the best of circumstances. But it is absolutely essential for someone in your position. You have nothing to be arrogant about. The trick is to learn to be humble without being "self-reproachful." You are not in a position to demand anything from anybody. An arrogant, demanding attitude of entitlement will not avail you anything. In fact, it will alienate rather than attract people who are willing to help you. No one owes you anything. The best you can hope for is a chance to make it, not a guarantee of success. Do not think you are too good to take a menial job, even if on paper you are over qualified for it. Remember, "Your head is in the mouth of the lion" – and as someone put it, "When your head is in the mouth of the lion you, do not jerk it out" – or antagonize him.

Act Like You Want Something Out of Life

Watch the good football players. When they are hit they rarely fall backwards. Instead, they fall forward. I submit that the reason is not just athleticism, but also attitude. They want the yardage or score more than the defender who is trying to stop them wants to keep them out of the end zone.

If you want to be successful you need the same desire and determination. If you act like you do not care or "tip toe" through the holes of opportunity, you will get stopped in your tracks. You have to want something in life to get it.

A friend tells a story about one of his brothers whom he tried to help. My friend helped him get an apartment and some furniture. But his brother did not keep his end of the deal. He would not help pay the bills. When the responsible brother reproached his sibling, he cursed and said he never told him he "wanted a d — thing and that the things that were obtained for his benefit were not his idea."

The moral of this story is that if you do not want anything, no one can make you have it. That is true of education and many other things that will improve the quality of your life.

Expect to Get What You Want

Educators have known for a long time that there is a close connection between high achievement and expectations. In the literature, this phenomenon is known as the "Pygmalion effect."[17] One of the quickest ways to get going in the right direction and do well is have high expectations for yourself even if no one else does. When people find out that you are an ex-inmate they are likely to immediately underestimate you. In other words, they will not expect much from you and will think you will do something stupid and get sent back to prison. In matters of race this is what President George W. Bush calls "the soft bigotry of low expectations." It happens in virtually every area of life.

If no one expects anything out of you, you must hold yourself to high standards and expectations. The reason is that there is something powerful about expecting the best and expecting to be successful. It is one of the surest ways to transform a negative situation into a positive experience.

When children at my church try to sell me Girl Scout cookies, I can tell the novices who are not used to making a sales pitch. They usually say, "You don't want to buy any cookies do you?" Since I do not need to eat them at my weight, that gives me an easy way out by saying "no." But I try to make it a learning experience for them. I supplement my response by saying, "I do not want to buy any cookies, but I might if you tell me why I should buy them from you."

What this reveals is that the kids did not expect to succeed in selling cookies or they have been told "no" so much they have become discouraged. The point of this is that if you do not expect to succeed, why should anyone else think you can? If you do not think you can do a particular thing and do it well no one else will.

4.5 SELF-ESTEEM

Know Who You Are

You are somebody. You were made in the image of God. While the *imageo dei*, image of God, in you might have been effaced, there is a good person behind the facade of skin trying to get out. As a person who was made in God's image you are already somebody – regardless of your situation or status in life.

Talk to Yourself, But be Careful about What You Say

Do not tell yourself negative things. You will hear enough negative things from other people. Learn to think in positive terms. It is amazing to see how what we think tends to determine what comes to us. The reason is that behavior follows what we think. If you stop telling yourself negative things, you will be less likely to do them.

Improve Yourself

Develop a plan for making yourself better. At a minimum, it should include reading one or more good newspapers, novels, magazines and the "good book"– the Bible as sacred texts of your faith. When you encounter words you do not understand, look them up, add them to your vocabulary and use them in grammatically correct sentences. People will be impressed with your command of the language and this will not only help you get a decent job, but also make you feel better about yourself. Nothing will help you make a better first impression than good communication skills.

Realize That High Self-Esteem is a By-Product of Doing Good

Understand that self-esteem is related to what you do with your life. The best way to feel good about yourself is do something worthwhile with your life instead of negative things that undermine your sense of self-esteem. Realizing your purpose for being here produces a natural high and your self-esteem will soar when you begin to act in accordance with it.

Don't Lose Your Butt Trying To Save Your Face

One of the biggest problems for a lot of young men is their belief that they have to respond with violence when they are "dissed." Some think it is the only way to save face. When their perverted sense of honor is offended, they think the only way to respond is with force – even deadly force. How many people do you know who, in an effort to save their face, lost their freedom, health, family, or life? Everything they worked for and everything their parents hoped for went down the drain in one fell swoop because they cared more about what somebody thought who didn't even care about them than the folk who had their best interest at heart. Self respect depends more on you than anyone else. If you feel good about yourself, there is nothing that anyone can say that will make you angry enough to "go off the deep end." Respect yourself, and others will, too.

4.6 HAPPINESS

Find Fulfillment Where Everybody Else Finds It—Giving

Fulfillment does not come from getting or taking, but giving. That is the flaw in the hip-hop culture that glorifies thuggery and prison life. People far wiser than you or I have learned that "a life is made by what we get, but a living is made by what we give."[18] A pre-occupation with "bling" or money that adheres to the philosophy which says, "Get rich through any means necessary or die trying," will put you on the fast track back to jail, prison, or an early grave. The Bible is right, "For the love of money is a root of all kinds of evil." (I Tim. 6:10 NKJV). If you need stuff or the things money can buy to make you feel powerful or important, the issue with which you are dealing is self-esteem, not happiness. Besides, the emphasis that is often placed on being happy in our culture does not reflect the reality of life as Paul Lawrence Dunbar puts it:

A crust of bread and a corner to sleep in,
A minute to smile and an hour to weep in,
A pint of joy to a peck of trouble,
And never a laugh but the mourns come double...[19]

The Bible speaks about happiness a lot, but it says much more about suffering and self denial. There are some things we just have to "grin and bear."

There are only two kinds of people in the world: "givers and takers." Your life will improve when you become a giver and stop being a taker. Far greater happiness will be found in becoming a person who gives, rather that one who is always receiving or taking.

Don't Postpone Your Happiness

There is a lot to be said for learning to delay gratification. Some things need to be put off until the time is right. That is called delaying gratification.

But that should not include personal happiness. Your happiness or contentment should not be put off until you get out of trouble – or until you save enough money from honest work, learn a trade, earn a degree, get married, or some other event takes place. Marcus Aurelius observed centuries ago that "very little is needed to make life happy." He said, "It is within yourself, in your way of thinking."[20] Many people get in trouble by stealing or robbing because they think money will make them happy.

Some people "sing because they are happy." But if you wait until you are happy you may not ever sing. The truth is that you can sing yourself happy. You do not have to wait until you feel happy. If that were necessary, there are few people who would ever experience it.

Making the best of every day is the key. There is a gift in your present circumstances that cannot be unwrapped in the future, but little by little each day. Besides, you do not live in the future – but the here and now. When you get up every morning you should say, "This is the day the Lord has made and I will be glad in it!" (Psalm 118:24 NKJV).

You can have contentment, peace, and happiness where you are right now. Most of us live our lives some place other than where we are. There is an art to being where you are without always trying to live in some other time, place, or circumstance. If you are not happy with who you are as a person, where you live or what you possess will not make you happy.

Paul, a famous biblical prisoner, said, "I've learned in whatever state I am in to be content." (Phil. 4:11 NKJV). The key is acceptance of yourself and your circumstances. Remember the Serenity Prayer: "God grant me the serenity to accept the things I cannot change…"[21]

4.7 DREAMS

Rediscover and Act on Your Dreams

In his poem entitled "Dream Deferred," Langston Hughes asked:

What happens to a dream deferred?
Does it dry up
like a raisin in the sun?

Or fester like a sore
And then run?
Does it stink like rotten meat?

Or crust and sugar over
like a syrupy sweet?

Maybe it just sags
like a heavy load.

Or does it explode?[22]

It is possible that you are in the predicament you are in now because you either deferred your dream or completely abandoned it.

You did not set out to become a prisoner. You had a dream of doing something special with your life. A prison record may make it harder to accomplish your dream now or it could, as it did in the case of Joseph, serve as a stepping stone. It is up to you.

When Joseph ended up in jail through no fault of his own, he never got bitter. He was sustained by his dream of greatness. (Genesis Chapters 37-45 NKJV). While his brothers mocked him and his father was less than encouraging, he held onto his dream. Through the adversity of being thrown in a pit and languishing in Pharaoh's prison, he was undoubtedly sustained by the assurance of God's presence on which he depended to make his dream a reality.

It is true, "the bigger the dream, the greater its power to motivate." That was evident in the life of Moses. After he killed a man and went into exile, God spoke to him forty years later and reaffirmed his plan for his life. Although you have lost a lot of time in jail, it is not necessarily wasted. It might just be that God was getting you ready for something for which you were not yet prepared. This may be your time! Build on it!

Avoid learned helplessness. You are not hopeless. You have options. Seize them by taking the initiative to live your life fully. Do not continue to be a victim. Become the victor – now. When you were young, you had hopes and dreams for your life. You wanted to be somebody special. Whether it is too late to realize them depends upon you. It may be necessary to adjust your dreams to your current circumstances, but it is still possible for you to do something positive with your life.

What happened to your dream?

4.8 THINKING

Question Conventional Wisdom

One of the most important skills you can master is thinking, especially for yourself. That means learning to question what is passed off as wisdom. For example, the conventional wisdom is that a person should not burn his or her bridges. But that is not always true. If you want to go back to where you have always been, the best way to get there is to travel the same old paths that always led you to a dead end. Getting to a better place may require you to go in a different direction.

Practically, that may mean avoiding some people or ending some friendships. As

Dan Aviely suggests, some doors need to be closed because it is possible to keep them open too long. That is also true of the bridges we hang on to. Our problem is reluctance to limit our options because, as Aviely puts it, "We cannot stand the idea of closing the doors on our alternatives!"[23] When you hang on to false friends and keep bad company that is what you are doing.

Perhaps the best example of this phenomenon is the experience of the Chinese commander named Xiang Yu who led his forces into battle in 310 BC. While his troops were resting for the night, he set the ships on fire they had used to cross the Yangtze River and ordered that all their cooking utensils be destroyed. He told his undoubtedly bewildered soldiers that without the pots and ships "they had no other choice but to fight their way to victory or perish." This caused them to focus their energies and efforts on winning so completely that they won nine consecutive victories.[24]

When you close doors you are dramatically increasing your chance of being successful in the most important battle of your life – the battle to stay out of prison! The "convict code" that might have served you well behind bars is counter productive in the real world. That is another form of conventional wisdom that must be questioned. As I heard a correctional officer at a local jail put it, "life is a lot like a jail in the sense that when one door closes another one opens." In a jail or prison no two doors are open at the same time and before one opens, the one you walked through must be closed.

Reflect on Your Life Experience

To stay out of the situation that got you in trouble, think about it. The object is not to figure out how to do it without getting caught. Rather, it is to learn the lesson that will benefit you on your journey towards wholeness and rehabilitation. The only way to avoid it in the future is to be aware of it. Nothing on which you stumbled before should trip you up again – if you are smart! Too many people have experiences that they have failed to learn from and in the process, not only retard their growth, but also expose themselves to unnecessary pain. The grandmother of one of my friends told him, "If a dog bites you one time it's an accident, but if he bites you again, you just like getting dog bit."

Think Outside of the Cell Block

People in unfavorable circumstances or trying to solve a difficult problem are often advised to "think outside of the box." Ordinarily, I take issue with this advice on the ground that if one is in a bad place he or she not only needs to think outside of it, but also get out of it and "act out of it."

If you are in jail, however, that is not possible yet. For you, thinking outside of the cell block is the next best thing. This is a necessary prelude to getting out. The last thing you need is a cell block mentality when you get out of jail or prison. You will be on your own outside. You cannot let people who do not care about you influence you to do things that will get you thrown back in prison! The easiest way to do that is let the bad habits and associates that got you incarcerated in the first place and allowed you to survive in jail continue to guide the way you function in society. An entirely new skill set is needed outside of jail or prison. It begins by getting rid of "stinking thinking." "Stinking thinking" leads to stinking conduct that prevents you from learning how to act outside the box – or cell block.

Use Your Head for Something Other Than a Hat Rack

If you do not think for yourself, someone else will. The problem is that they are not likely to have your best interest at heart. Think! There is no substitute for doing that. Remember that everything in life has a cost and consequences. In love and life, all of us are at some time or another somebody's fool. Whose fool you become ought not to be anybody's choice but yours. For many of your peers, you will be considered a fool for loving your wife and children, going to church, and working a hard job. Stand, even if you must stand alone for a time! The end result is well worth it.

Don't Use your Body as a Canvas for Someone Else's Art

For some people, getting a tattoo is almost a rite of passage. For some, they are a "fashion statement" and a way of identifying with a particular group or culture.

Removing tattoos can not only be costly, but also uncomfortable and time consuming. But the cost and discomfort probably pale when the psychic pain associated with remorse over their presence is considered. That occurs when the circumstances that led to the tattoo have changed. An example of this is the break-up of a personal relationship or divorce. In a word, tattooing a fiancé's name on a visible part of your body can create problems as you transition from one phase of life to another.[25] The same thing occurs when you out-grow the need to be a gang member or overcome alcoholism or drug addiction. What you put on your body under the influence of drugs or alcohol may come back to haunt you in the form of rejection by potential suitors or employers. At a minimum it can be a source of embarrassment.

If you are "into" self expression, why not write poems instead of using your body as a canvas for a tattoo artist? You should resist the urge to get a tattoo, especially one on any part of your body that identifies you as a gang member or a former prison inmate on any part of your body. A tattoo that contains a racist symbol like a swastika should also be avoided. I saw a photograph of a young man with his entire face and neck covered with tattoos that included swastikas. If you just have to get a tattoo, do not put it on your wrists, hands, neck or face. It will be hard enough for you to get a job. Why make your life harder than it needs to be by telling people more of your past than is necessary? Where you have been is nothing to be ashamed of if you are trying to overcome it through positive changes in your life. Nor is it something to brag about or be proud of. That is what visible tattoos that reveal your past criminal activity may say to potential employers—that you are proud of your jail record.

Besides, tattoos let people read your mind without you ever saying a word, even after you have changed the way you think. This makes it easy for people to judge you on the basis of a stereotype.

Use Your Imagination

I watch with amazement the athleticism of basketball players who hone their skills on neighborhood playgrounds that are then showcased in college and professional sport arenas. Their "game" includes not only the ability to shoot, but also "penetrate" defenses with imaginative moves and contortions of their bodies.

I saw a child in a housing project dribbling a basketball by himself hour after hour. He dribbled with both hands and then through his legs, without looking down and with little effort. That is how anyone gets good at doing anything in life – practice!
Just think what would happen if the same energy is applied to the development and implementation of an imaginative life-strategy. As great moves in sports are designed in an athlete's mind, so are the plans of successful people in the real world. The best move you can make now is to go to school, go to church, and work on your character. As an athlete is not able to execute unusual moves without having to practice and without the ability to see himself doing it, more constructive pursuits off the court must also begin with the imagination. It is true, "What you can conceive, you can achieve." But, if you can not see yourself in a different light or a better role, you are not likely to even attempt, let alone accomplish it. That is why it is so important to understand that you still have options and that you can do something about your situation, if you will. Do not allow what you have been through to steal your hope of a better life.

Work On Your Mind

State penal systems are euphemistically called "the Department of Corrections." The reality is that they are departments of punishment. There is a difference between discipline and punishment. Correction only occurs when the individual involved makes up his or her mind to amend his or her ways in response to the right stimuli. That is a matter of choice. One can choose to do what is right or socially acceptable or continue a life of crime for which the state will always provide a jail or prison cell. One's mind is the one thing over which he or she has absolute control, regardless of where he or she may be. The state can lock a person up in a cell and either hold or throw away the key. But each person controls the key to his or her mind. Through reading, for example, you can travel the world from behind bars. You can think the loftiest thoughts from the lowest place on earth. What you do with your mind is up to you. As The College Fund's slogan puts it, "A mind is a terrible thing to waste."[26] All of this indicates that you have far more control of your future than you realize., even though your past will always influence your present and future until you decide to do something about it.

Get Some Coaching

People who are successful in business, for example, do not know everything. They buy the expertise they need from lawyers, accountants, or other professionals – depending on the nature of their activity. People who are sick go to physicians. Troubled people seek counselors (drug, alcohol, mental health). Authors of books hire editors. Entertainers hire managers and publicists. Professional athletes hire coaches. As good as Tiger Woods is in golf, he has a coach.

Moral: Get some help. You do not have to know everything. Instead, have the humility to recognize that simple truth, and exercise the good judgment to get the help you need. Admitting that you need help is the first step. That does not mean that you are weak, but that you are smart.

Get In Touch With Thoughts You May Not Be Aware Of

Now that you are free or about to be free, "Are you sure you can handle it?" For some, freedom is more challenging than incarceration. That may be the reason some people unwittingly keep committing crimes after their release from prison and sabotage their lives.

In *Escape from Freedom*,[27] Erich Fromm suggests that one of the means that people use to escape from freedom is "destructiveness" that is "rooted in the unbearable individual powerlessness and isolation." In our culture no one experiences this more than a parolee or ex-inmate. Think about it! Are you running from something? Regardless of how hard your life was on the outside, it was better than being in prison because as Thomas Fuller observed, "Lean liberty is better than fat slavery."[28] The sad truth is that many of you like having someone make decisions for you, the security of having a place to stay and something to eat, and not having to work and pay bills. In addition, there is someone to protect you from yourself. Some are more afraid of themselves than they are of others. You probably get better healthcare in prison than you could afford outside, if you are like most people I know. If you think this is a good situation, there is something wrong with you. Until you get to a point of accepting responsibility for yourself, your rehabilitation is not complete.

Think Like A Free Person

According to Mahatma K. Gandhi, "The moment the slave resolves that he will no longer be a slave his fetters fall. He frees himself and shows the way to others. Freedom and slavery are mental states."[29]

In a similar vein, Angela Y. Davis said, "We have to talk about liberating minds as well as liberating society."[30] This is a process that has to begin long before a person is released from prison. For most people it begins when they realize that liberty has limits. No one is free to do whatever he pleases. Learning to live within the constraints set by law begins in your mind a long time before it shows up in a disciplined life characterized by the ability to say no to yourself and peers.

Thinking like a free person is nothing less than choosing for yourself the life you want to live instead of depending on someone else to make decisions for you.

Guard Your Mind

As long as you do not cause any problems, I doubt that anyone in authority cares what you feel or think. But it is critically important for you. Consequently, as those in authority guard your body, you must guard your mind, emotions, and spirit. If you fail in this task, destruction will be the outcome of your time in jail. If you let the negative influences to which you are exposed get in your head you will in effect impose on yourself an intellectual life sentence that you will continue to serve long after you have served your time behind bars. You decide what will enter your mind. What you let into your mind is the key to how the rest of your life turns out.

On one of my few attempts to play golf on a windy day, my coach kept saying, "Don't let the wind get in your head." That is good advice in every area of life. What gets in your head determines how you handle your challenges. Solomon noticed this centuries ago when he said, "As a man thinks so is he." (Prov. 33:7 NKJV).

A sentinel needs to stand guard over your mind with the authority and power to stop every unwanted intruder. These include revenge, hate, aggression, guilt, self-pity, blame, unforgiveness, perversion, narcissism, complacency, evil, laziness, and the like. Do not allow them to get in your head. If that happens they will influence everything you do.

Think Like A Bee

Muhammad Ali used to say, "float like a butterfly, sting like a bee." The humble bee is an example of how you should think. It models not just possibility thinking, but also possibility acting. It is one thing to think you can do something, but another to do it. That a bumble bee can fly is amazing. Its body is not sleek, but almost oval in appearance. Its wings are small and out of proportion to its body. From an aerodynamic perspective, there is little to suggest that it can fly. The only problem is nobody ever told it that flight was beyond its capabilities – and it manages to fly in spite of itself and what others think. With this approach to life, you can also do more than your circumstances might suggest you are capable of doing. It begins when you stop thinking about what you "can't" do and start doing what you can! Do not let what others think you can or cannot do limit your possibilities or options. Eventually, as the poet reminds us, the person who accomplishes anything is the person who "thinks he can."

4.9 RESPONSIBILITY

Beware of the Blame Game

Blaming "the man" is a waste of time. Nobody keeps you down but yourself. Consequently, you can choose to get up anytime you want to.

Do not see yourself as a victim, but a victor. Blaming others just delays the search for hard solutions to your problems and the effort that you must make to change your life.

If you ever get into the mode of blaming some one for your problems, look in the mirror. You have been your worst enemy. You have done more to mess up your life than anyone else. That is why finger pointing is such a futile exercise. The object of this observation is not to make you feel guilty. Guilt is another form of imprisonment. Rather, it is to encourage you to avoid shifting blame and avoiding responsibility for making the improvements in yourself that only you can make.

Tend to Your Own Business

Do not ask a spouse, parent or friend to do for you what you ought to do for yourself. Whether it is reporting to a probation or parole officer or paying fines, take care of it yourself. You got yourself in the mess you are in. Not them. Do not ask family members, especially children, to lie for you by calling an employer or probation officer to say you are sick when you are not.

Be Responsible

There is a relationship between how you act in every area of life and your understanding of what it means to be responsible. If you are irresponsible in your use of alcohol, for example, that mindset is likely to show up in your relationships with members of the opposite sex. If you are not responsible in managing your money, you are not likely to be any better in matters of morals. Getting it together, as they say, is a total package. Becoming a new person requires you to work on and succeed at being responsible in every area of your life because failure in any one of them can keep you from reaching your goals. How many times have you known people who are smart in terms of academics but lose in the game of life because they fathered babies they couldn't or wouldn't support and got thrown in jail for failing to pay child support? What about those who go to work at an honest job, but get into trouble because they can't stop beating their girlfriends or wives?

A lot of stress and anxiety occur when you lose control of your thoughts. Thinking positive, wholesome thoughts will help. Paul undoubtedly had this in mind when he said:

"Whatever things are true, whatever things are noble, whatever things are just, whatever things are pure, whatever things are lovely, whatever things are of good report; if there is any virtue, and if there is any praiseworthy – meditate on these things." (Phil. 4:8 NKJV).

4.10 CONFLICT

Deal With Conflict in the Right Way

Conflict is not necessarily a bad thing. It confirms the worth of what you want in life. If what people seek was of no value there would never be conflict. The problem is that everything you want of value, someone else wants it too. What determines whether you get it or someone else? Ultimately, the answer is you – your attitude, intelligence, skills, character, and ability. There is absolutely no reason in the world why you should not get what you want out of life without having to kill or commit a crime to get it. This involves knowing how to talk to people and how to negotiate. Getting loud or using force will not avail you much in civilized society. The greatest rewards are in resolving conflict in a way that is socially acceptable. It is absolutely essential for you to learn how to "disagree without being disagreeable."

Look at how you once handled conflict. Make sure you understand why that was wrong and what is appropriate now. Having a "short fuse" or "flying off the handle" will lead to the mismanagement of conflict. Remember what worked in prison does not avail you anything except trouble in conventional society.

Negotiation is an important skill. Learn it, because everything you want outside is obtained through this means – not fighting and scams. It is also an important conflict resolution process that will obviate the need to fight to appear to be strong or to get respect in the real world as opposed to what the "convict code" required you to do to survive in prison.

4.11 CHANGE

Make Small Changes

You can not possibly overcome your deficits at one time. They did not come into existence overnight and cannot be remedied overnight. What is not impossible is getting on a path that will lead in that direction. As "a journey of a thousand miles begins with the first step," personal change is a "cinch by the inch." On the other hand, expecting too much of yourself and others will lead to discouragement. Remember the Serenity Prayer, which asks God for, among other things, "the courage to change the things that I can."[31]

Change The Way You See Yourself

There will be many people who will not think well of you just because you have a "C" on your record. But in the final analysis, how your life turns out from this point forward depends more on what you think about yourself than what others think. It is good to have someone who believes in you. But if you do not think you can succeed, why should anyone else? The Bible that you probably threw away a long time ago has some wonderful instructions on how you should see yourself. For example, Solomon, one of the wisest men to ever live, said: "For as he thinks in his heart, so is he" (Prov. 23:7 NKJV). When Joshua was preparing to go into the promised land, some of his spies brought back a negative report concerning their chance of success. A majority said the people who live in the land are giants and they were as grasshoppers relative to them. This calls to mind the observation of Eleanor Roosevelt that "no one can make you feel inferior without your permission." The reason is that you are in charge of your mind. You can choose your attitude and outlook on life like the minority group of spies who said the land is flowing with milk and honey and they were well able to take it. (Num. 13:28-30 NKJV). The difference was that instead of an obstacle, they saw an opportunity. This is called possibility thinking. Again, the Bible encourages this through its emphasis on faith and the promise that all things are possible to the person who believes. (St. Mark 9:23 NKJV).

Act Like a Butterfly

The possibility of change is programmed into us in utero, long before we leave the security of our mother's womb. Perhaps the best example of this process of change known as metamorphosis is a butterfly. Charles Colson eloquently described it in these words:

> The butterfly is nature's most
> visible illustration of rebirth. Once drab
> and earth bound as a caterpillar, the
> butterfly emerges from its cocoon in
> beautifully radiant colors, soaring
> upward into the sky. Free-Born Again – just as
> each of us can be when we are, through Christ, born
> again in the spirit.[32]

Prison can be the cocoon that allows you to be transformed from a worm into a beautiful butterfly. You do not have to come out of prison worse than you went in. It can change you for the better if you follow good advice and place your life "under new management."

4.12 SELF

Don't Be a Fool

Everybody may be somebody's fool at some time or the other, but there is no need to do it on a regular basis. We have heard the saying, "God looks after babies and fools." All of us have been in both categories. Babies grow up. But some people never stop acting like a fool. Whether you are one of them is up to you.

By now you should have figured out what does and does not work. Someone defined insanity as "doing the same thing over and over and expecting a different result." If you continue to break the law, you are going to end up in the same place you have always been – jail or prison. If you are tired of what you are getting out of life, it is time to try doing something different – going straight! It is up to you. God is not going to do it for you, no matter how much you pray. Some things are under your control as a matter of divine delegation. How you live and the decisions you make are in that category.

Invest In Yourself

Someone wisely observed that "owning a thing is not an asset because it is on your "a..." The same can be said of the vehicle in which you ride or jewelry around your neck.

The best investment you can make is in yourself. Going to school, learning a trade, buying books, and attending seminars, for example, will pay a higher return on your labor and money than anything else on the market – including the lottery. The best investment I ever made was going to school. Education is still the greatest equalizer of the status of people our society has to offer.

Know the Enemy

Pogo was right: "We have met the enemy and it is us."[33] You have been your worst enemy. If you succeed in confronting yourself, defeating every other foe will be a piece of cake. As a young man discovered after successfully battling his demons, the problem was "in-me."

"Get Yourself Out of The Way"

Dealing with ourselves is one of the hardest things we will ever do. We can walk away from toxic family members and friends. But if we are the source of the toxicity, we carry it with us wherever we go. As some wag put it, our problem is that "we carry ourselves everywhere we go." Someone else said, "wherever I go, there I am." The serious point in this is that we cannot escape from ourselves. That places a premium on making sure that we are fit for ourselves to not just know, but also to spend time with. If you are good enough for yourself to know and spend time with, you will have a far easier time getting along with others without creating the problems that have so often wrecked your relationships in the past than you ever had before. Nathaniel Hawthorne was right, "For what other dungeon is so dark as one's own heart? What jailer is as inexorable as one's self?"[34]

Forget Your Self

It is not about you, despite what the narcissistic "me generation" says. I saw a sign in a local jail that so informed new arrivals. The sign read, "This is not Burger King––you will not have it your way." What the jailers meant was that the "inmates," were not going to run "the asylum." Let me let you in on a little secret. Regardless of whether you are entering jail or prison or leaving to go home, the advice on the sign is equally applicable. You will have to conform to society's norms and expectations and not the other way around. Get used to it. That is the way it is for almost everybody else.

No-Fault Self-Improvement

The idea of fault is never far from the mind of most people. Whenever something bad happens, the first thing we say is, "It was not my fault." The psyche, especially those of people who are not functioning well, is always predisposed to assigning fault or blame.

I submit that we need to take a no-fault approach to our troubles–as we do in divorce and some aspects of insurance litigation. Regardless of how you got into a bad situation, it is up to you to get out of it.

4.13 TIME

Do Not Waste Time in Prison

As John C. Maxwell reminds us, *Robinson Crusoe* was written in prison; John Bunyan wrote *Pilgrim's Progress* in the Bedford jail; Sir Walter Raleigh wrote *The History of the World* during a thirteen year imprisonment. Luther translated the Bible while confined in the Castle of Wartburg.[35] Whether your experience is good or bad depends upon its effect on you, your attitude towards it, and whether you learn anything from it. These factors determine what you do with it and how you respond to it. If you make the best of it and the time is well spent, the lessons you learn will help guide your life in productive new directions.

Too often people say, "I don't have time," when asked about something constructive. But they have as much time as anyone else–24 hours a day. What people accomplish behind bars can be done outside of prison if they do not waste their time on things that do not matter.

The biggest waste of your time is blaming others for your mistake or making excuses for your failure. Do something constructive with the substance of your life. It is never too late to make a fresh start. Life does not have any signs saying "no U-turn allowed." You have wasted enough time already.

Seize the Moment

There is no time like now. The late Coach George Allen used to say, "The future is now."[36] The worst thing one can do is spend his or her life waiting on someone to do for him or her later what is within his or her power to accomplish now.

If you wait for your circumstances to be totally favorable, you will never get anything done in your life. There are times when you have to act. Some things are more a matter of timing than anything else. In baseball, for example, the outfielder who waits to see which way the ball is going will not catch it very often. The player who is good at this game is off at the crack of the bat. You cannot afford to wait until you are out of jail or prison. The time to start moving is NOW! He who hesitates is not only lost, but also unsuccessful in taking advantage of opportunities which often knock only once and move on.

Make Half Time Adjustments

If you have been in prison for any length of time, you have probably squandered the first half of your life. Although the temptation will be strong to think that the game of life is over for you, there is more time on the clock. The outcome of the struggle depends upon how the clock, with its precious minutes and seconds, is managed.

Deciding what to do with the second half of your life is as critical for you as it is for anyone else. As Peter Drucker observed, the "one prerequisite for managing the second half of your life" is that "you must begin long before you enter it." He says that this involves developing "parallel careers" and "a second major interest." This is part of what he calls "managing one's self."[37]

A smart person or team will learn from mistakes. In sports, the team that ultimately wins is often the one that is best at making half-time adjustments. That is the role of coaches – and a good reason for you to get the best possible advice on how to change your game plan. Too many people are satisfied with just letting the clock run out instead of trying to get back in the game. Remember that the game is not over until there is no more time left on the clock. Keep trying to score within the rules, regardless of the deficit you have to make up. Who knows? You may yet make a game of it!

PART III

Post-Release Life Planning: Where Do You Go From Here?

CHAPTER FIVE
Making the Right Moves

As we are not pawns on a giant chessboard that are moved or manipulated by the impersonal hand of fate, we have the capacity to determine how our lives turn out. In a sense, life is like a game of chess. The difference is that instead of pawns under someone else's control we are both pawns and players who have been empowered to make the moves that determine whether we win or lose in the game of life. The moves we make are up to each one of us. It is important for you to realize that you are not at someone else's mercy. In this chapter, I make suggestions that will help you make better moves than the ones that got you where you are now—and help you get out of the trap you have gotten into.

5.1 DEVELOP A GAME PLAN

In watching football games for a number of years, I have concluded that any game plan will work if it is faithfully executed. The same is true of formations, offensive strategies, and defensive schemes. On the other hand, the best of plans or systems will not produce good results if they are abandoned prematurely or poorly executed. In football as in life, "If a person fails to plan, he or she plans to fail." Very few good things in life will just fall into your lap—or happen because of good luck. Rather, it is "planning your work and working your plan" that makes the difference between success and failure. The harder you work to implement a good plan, the luckier you will become.

In order to make the best of your fresh start, you need an action plan for your life. Assuming you have dealt with the mental and spiritual issues discussed in Chapters One through Four, your plans at a minimum should include:

1. Finding a decent place to live. While it is good to be discriminating about where you live, you may have few choices in this matter because of limited income. My mother used to say, "Beggars can't be choosers." But to the extent you can, it is important that you avoid areas that will create a problem for you. In many areas in which you will have to live, there will be temptations a plenty. If you have learned your lesson, you will be able to walk away from them. No one will be able to keep you from doing something stupid but yourself—regardless of where you live. It is up to you.

As a general matter, living with family members or responsible friends for a limited time until you get a job will be better than a shelter. But take what you can get in the most wholesome environment available until you can do better.

2. Getting a job. Notice that I did not say a good job. Your options are likely to be limited at first. Any lawful work will let you get your foot in the door. The work ethic of people today is so poor that if you impress the employer with your willingness to work, by showing up, and with thoroughness in doing your job, you will be promoted because you will stand out. There is an advantage to being hungry. Be willing to give more and better service than you are paid for, to use the advice of the late Napoleon Hill.[1] People who have a job can always find a job. You have to start somewhere. Do not let your pride cause you to thumb your nose at a job that you can use as a stepping stone to a better position. It is all right to flip burgers if necessary. One fellow was heard to grumble when the only job he could get was riding on the back of a garbage truck, "Man, I can't let my women see me doing that."

3. Getting some help. If you have a substance abuse problem, do not try to handle it by yourself. If only as a preventive measure, get into a program that will help you stay clean. If there are mental health issues, it goes without saying that they, too, should be addressed. Most communities have mental health clinics that provide free or reduced fee services. Many churches have counseling and substance abuse programs. Do not be surprised if they have strict requirements and a no nonsense approach. If you want what they have to offer, realize that it will be on their terms, not yours.

4. Going Back to School. Ultimately how you handle the challenge of freedom is dependent upon the ability to get and keep a job that will pay you enough money to meet your obligations. For most ex-inmates, that will require going back to school. That is not unusual for any one today. No one ever finishes school. There are community colleges and vocational or technical schools everywhere that can help you find your niche. Many trades will pay a higher wage than jobs that allow you to wear a white shirt and tie. Which would you rather have, a prestigious position with inadequate pay or a trade that allows you to control your own destiny and support your family? If you want more than a job and have the motivation to achieve your goals, one of the first things you should investigate is educational options. In most communities there are community colleges and vocational schools that provide excellent programs for people like you.

5. Joining an accountability group. For some, that will be a church or mosque. Under no circumstances should it be a gang or some other anti-social group that requires you to surrender control of your mind as a condition of membership. Whatever you do, get into an accountability group that will hold you accountable for becoming the person you were meant to be. If you did not find God in prison, do not stop until you make His acquaintance. It is hard enough to make it in life under the best

of circumstances; but without faith in God, it is impossible. I know some of you are probably foolish enough to be angry with God for all kinds of perverted reasons and even blame him for the consequences of your bad decisions. You may be angry with the church because the pastor told you truth you were unable to hear or the members refused to let you use them. Get over it. They did you a favor, which you did not have sense enough to appreciate. You need their help, and you can be of help to them in fulfilling their mission of preventing what happened to you from happening to others. Do not go thinking you are going to be trusted to teach a youth group! Go to learn and serve when the opportunity presents itself.

There are many accountability groups. In some respects that is what a church is. Recognizing that you are accountable to someone other than yourself should be a lesson you have learned by now from your prison experience. All of us need to be held accountable because we do not always see things as clearly as we need to.

All of us need somebody we can depend on to always tell us the truth and help us correct "stinking thinking," and do reality testing. This is nothing short of help in telling the difference between "sugar" on the one hand and that which is malodorous waste on the other. Unfortunately, when we have smelled the malodorous stuff long enough, our ability to distinguish it from sugar may be impaired.

6. Getting some coaching. If the best athletes in the world need coaching to be the best that they can be, that is true of the rest of us in the ordinary pursuits of life. Sometimes this happens through mentoring relationships. We are sharpened through this process "as iron sharpens iron." (Prov. 27:17) That is what mentoring involves. There are folks who will tell us the hard truth because they see something in us. They are more valuable and unvarnished than those who tell us what we want to hear because of "the soft bigotry of low expectations." Having someone who can give guidance and good advice can make all the difference in how your life turns out. There are not many people who will take you on as a protégé if they are required to put you on their back and carry you. But if you give evidence of trying to help yourself, there are good people who will give you a hand up by serving as your mentor.

7. Dealing with broken relationships. Just because you paid your debt to society does not mean it has been paid to your family. Do not expect to walk back into your family's life as if nothing ever happened. Your spouse has been making all of the decisions and your children have been looking to him or her for the permission to go various places. This power will not be readily surrendered to you. Be prepared to have to earn it! You need to deal with the guilt you will experience in this area by not just seeking forgiveness, but also making amends for what you have done. Just saying you are sorry may not be enough. But it is a good start. After that, you will be on trial, whether you like it or not, to see whether you really meant it or whether it was just a ruse to continue to use and hurt people as you probably did in the past. So many times people say, "What I do only hurts me." That is not true because of the way we are related to others. That is the nature of a system. Every part affects the other parts.

There is no such thing as a "victimless crime." The jury will be out long after you get out of prison on these issues. Whether there is a yellow ribbon tied to the tree in front of your family's house depends very largely on you—and your attitude. They are not likely to relish welcoming the same old person who caused them nothing but pain and grief. Now, a changed man or woman is another matter.

If you threw away your family through abuse of alcohol, drugs, and infidelity, do not think that everyone will be glad to see you. You have hurt and disappointed people—probably all of your life. If you had not been put on "ice" for a while, your destructive pattern would have continued until you got into even worse trouble or someone killed you. Sometimes we have to thank God even for something as unpleasant as time in prison. If you, as the prodigal son did in his pig pen, come to yourself, prison will have been the best thing that ever happened to you. Paul was right: "All things work together for good to those who love God, to those who are the called according to His purpose" (Rom. 8:28 NKJV). The same point was made by Ralph Waldo Emerson in his "Essay on Compensation."[2] There is good in every situation. The lowly oyster makes pearls by secreting a substance around an irritating grit of sand. What you do with your irritants will make all the difference in how your life turns out.

All of us have a calling. Finding yours is one of the ways to success in life. Your calling may be as simple as being a father to your children—and a husband or wife to your spouse—and a priest to your family. Do not start over wrong by "shacking." That is part of the old irresponsible pattern of using people and being irresponsible that got you in trouble in the first place. A person who is irresponsible in something as simple and basic as this is likely to be the same way in every other area of his or her life. Too many of our women are being exploited and disrespected through meretricious relationships. If a woman is good enough for you to sleep with and father children by, she should be good enough for you to marry. I know an old man who used to tell his sons not to get involved with someone they would not want to marry. That is still good advice. What Gore Vidal said in 1968 still rings true: "To bring into the world an unwanted human being is as antisocial an act as murder."[3] That is why I contend that how you behave in private sexual relations is a pretty good indication of the course of your rehabilitation. What is even worse is that it is clear that children who grow up fatherless are more likely to get into trouble, have babies out of wedlock, get addicted to drugs,[4] and on and on, ad nauseum. Many young men in Youth Development Centers have one thing in common: they are angry with their fathers. Do not let your children become numbered among them. Once you are out of jail or prison:

> Adopt a lawful purpose or goal.
> Develop a plan to reach your goals. Without a plan, it is just a pipe dream.
> Work your plan.

In planning your life on the outside, you need to make provision for times of discontent and defeat which are sure to come when things go in unexpected ways, when you can not get opportunities which you are qualified for because of your record, and society makes you pay a debt you thought you had paid by throwing up your past to you, and shutting doors in your face. How will you handle these times? It cannot be done without the help of God and the encouragement of family members and friends. That is why, at a minimum, you should spare no effort to rebuild a relationship with God and members of your family.

5.2 CHOICES

Counting the Cost of Choices

One of the more interesting new ways of looking at crime is called "rational choice theory." It is based on the assumption that people are rational. According to the economists who are now using it to explain behavior, rationality is defined as follows: Rational people respond to incentives: When it becomes more costly to do something, they will tend to do it less; when it becomes easier, cheaper, or more beneficial, they will tend to do it more. In weighing their choices they will bear in mind the overall constraints upon them: not just the costs and benefits of a specific choice...And they will also consider the future consequences of present choices.[5]

There is little doubt that we make "complex calculations of costs and benefits when we act rationally, but we often do it unconsciously.[6] It is a way to anticipate likely consequences of our actions.[7] Applying these ideas to crimes leads to the conclusion that:

If crime rates are high in some areas, then rational choice theory says that crime must pay in those areas: We need to look for a way of raising the cost or lowering the benefits of committing crime.[8]

One does not have to think about this insight long to realize its potential to not only explain anti-social conduct but also come up with possible crime prevention strategies. The basic idea is that "when the costs or benefits of something change, people change their behavior."[9] This may explain why brawny bullies only pick on ninety-pound weaklings instead of kids their own size. It also may explain so-called black on black crime. Historically, the consequences of choosing black victims have not been as severe as they have been when the victim is of another race. This suggests that the easiest way to solve this problem is for law enforcement officials and judges to raise the cost of the behavior by ensuring that criminals who prey on members of their race will be treated just as harshly as they are when the victim is of another race.

Hate crime laws, and laws designed to protect children, for example, raise the cost of certain kinds of criminal conduct. By the same token, increasing police visibility and passing laws which encourage citizens to arm themselves and become the eyes of the police raise the cost of committing crimes. People are afraid. When people live in fear, they are dangerous to potential criminals because they refuse to be victims. For this reason, if you continue your criminal career, not only are you at risk of going back to jail, but you also are at risk of getting shot or killed. State legislators have increased this risk by passing laws that allow homeowners to shoot first and ask questions later. Georgia has joined other states in allowing licensed gun owners to take their guns into public places, including those that serve alcohol. This not only makes people feel more safe from crime, it also raises the risk for the criminal—and innocent bystanders.

While this theory is interesting, the promising conclusions of behavioral economists seem to be contradicted by statistics which show American prisons are overflowing as a result of decades of "get tough" laws which were designed to raise the cost of committing crime. It is possible to argue that these policies succeeded only in raising the cost of incarcerating people. But on the other hand, it is possible to contend that in a permissive and morally impoverished society based on the post modernist philosophy which denies the existence of moral absolutes, the jail population would be even higher in the absence of a crack down on crime because criminals "respond to the risks and costs of punishment."[10] Sadly, it is also possible to argue that the people who make up the huge prison population are those who were just too irrational to understand the implications of changes in the law that made it easier for them to be convicted and given long sentences because of mental illness or drug addiction.

Realize That You Reap What You Sow

It is paradoxical, but in order to receive you have to first give. Even the Bible affirms this truth: "It is more blessed to give than to receive" (Acts 20:35 NKJV). The key to receiving is giving.

This principle is the basis of much of scripture and is called the law of the harvest, seedtime, or seed sowing. "He who sows sparingly will also reap sparingly, and he who sows bountifully will also reap bountifully" (II Cor. 9:6 NKJV). It is universally true that one reaps what he or she sows in proportion to what is sown. One always, in other words, reaps what is sown (Gal. 6:7 NKJV).

Sow good, and good comes back to you. Sow evil, and evil comes back to you. Sow love, and love is what you receive. The same is true of hate, violence, or anything else. When bad things happen to you, it is not always a matter of bearing a cross. Sometimes it is "reaping a crop." One can not plant corn and get collards! So it is with everything you do.

Get Out of Your Penitentiary

Henry Van Dyke wrote: "I turned an ancient poet's book and found upon the page, 'stone walls do not a prison make or iron bars a cage."[11]

The worst prison or jail you can get thrown into is the one you make for yourself. It is more secure than any place the state can build. Forgiveness is the key that unlocks its doors—and the only way to shorten your time behind its impregnable bars. You need to get out of the penitentiary you have created long before you get out of the prison or jail where you have been sentenced. Ivan Illich observed that "in a consumer society there are inevitably two kinds of slaves; the prisoner of addiction and the prisoner of envy."[12]

Whenever you get outside of the walls of your prison, you are still not free until you break the shackles that bind your mind. Hating someone, having an unforgiving spirit, and seeking revenge mean that you are still not free. You get free when you forgive not only those you think wronged you, but also yourself. Corrie Tenboom says she did not get free of her concentration camp until she forgave the guard who humiliated her and contributed to the death of her sister.[13]

Leaving prison is perhaps the most daunting task you will ever undertake. It is, in the words of Walter Bruggeman, an exodus.[14] That is the word which was used to describe the exit of God's people from their bondage in Egypt that began with a "cry for freedom."

As leaving prison is like the experience of the Israelites in leaving slavery, so too is it like the uncertainty of their journey to the Promised Land and the wilderness they went through to reach it. The challenge of the wilderness includes the absence of any "visible means of support." It is important under these circumstances to remember that even if you are in the wilderness, you are not of it—and that it is a necessary step on your way to the place which you are destined for.[15] The discomforts of a wilderness experience are risked and accepted in response to the promise of a better life. This is nothing less than the resurrection to which each person who is at ease in bondage is called when he or she forsakes bondage in search of freedom even when it leads to a wilderness experience. For all its privation, the wilderness is preferable to bondage and nothing that is experienced in it should tempt you to want to go back to the place of your former bondage.

Face Facts

If you believe the system is unfair or racist, it does not make sense to put yourself under its control by engaging in criminal conduct. The fact is that you are where you are because of a poor decision you made—no one else. As John Hagee says, "You cannot change what you will not confront."[16] That means facing up to your situation and the reason you are in it.

If you believe that you are a political prisoner because judges and other politicians get elected by issuing tough sentences and building jails to protect people who are afraid of you, it is foolish to put yourself in a position for that to happen. As they say, "If you do not do the crime, you will not have to do the time."

Refuse to Be a Recidivist

There is no incentive for private prisons to make you more valuable. You are of most value when you make many returns to prison. If you stay the same, you simply provide a continuing supply of grist for the prison mill. That is not in society's interest. But it will guarantee a return on the investment that is made by corporations that are investing in prisons. The things that make you more valuable are:

1. Education
2. Marketable skills
3. Work ethic
4. Good character

Human beings can be recycled through a process of transformation. Recycling adds value to refuse by:

Reclaiming it from the garbage pile;
Changing it to a usable form; and
Re-using it for another purpose.

You can change yourself; but you can not change anybody else. Peace comes from this realization. This is the genius of the Serenity Prayer attributed to Reinhold Niebuhr:

God grant me the serenity to accept things I
cannot change, the courage to change the
things I can and the wisdom to know the difference.[17]

You cannot change the prison system, your family, or any other person. But you can change yourself—how you feel, what you think or believe, and how you behave. No one can do it but you. Whether you change depends on you. Recidivism indicates that you did not learn anything from being in prison, that you have not changed, and that you have not been rehabilitated. The key to not becoming a recidivist is avoidance of recidivist thinking and criminal behavior.

Learn the Difference Between Sugar and B.S.

People will approach you with all kinds of propositions. You will need to use all five of your senses to evaluate them and sort them out. If all else fails, put what you are offered to the smell test. That is why old folk used to tell their children they need to be able to tell the difference between sugar and sh—. With a little practice, you will be able to smell b.s. a mile away—long before someone offers it to you. Unfortunately some people just like things that do not smell good. Well has the Scripture said, "The dog returns to its vomit and the sow returns to the mire." I met a man who came into a lot of money. When his guardian moved him to a prestigious side of town, he was miserably unhappy. In agreeing to take him back to his old stomping grounds she contemptuously observed that his problem was that he "loved the smell of sh—" even though he could live anywhere he wanted to live.

The other side of this principle is, do not think you can b.s. your way through life. Do not be the purveyor of b.s. People who do that are eventually found out. Trying to b.s. your way through life is an indication that you have not learned anything from your prison experience. It also says to people who are wise to b.s. that you are still trying to "get over on them."[18]

The best policy is to tell the truth and stop trying to be slick. Get real. A genuine person is infinitely more valuable than one who is artificial or counterfeit.

Do A Personal Inventory

Look at what you have to work with. You may be surprised to find that you have far more assets than you thought. Think of the life skills you have acquired over the years. List your talents and abilities. The key to success is matching your interests and abilities with the job. If you are not satisfied that you have what it takes, go back to school.

Understand That Freedom Is a Choice

Freedom is not for everybody. Not everybody can handle its responsibilities and demands. Those who would be free must demonstrate the capacity to govern themselves. It requires self-control and self-discipline. It involves doing right without someone standing guard over you with a gun to make you behave. It is a matter of doing well because it works and is in your best interest.

You have the capacity to be free in your mind, feelings, and spirit even while behind bars. The person whose mind is free may know more freedom in jail or prison than people on the streets who allow themselves to become negative, and believe that how his or her life turns out is the result of forces and people beyond his or her control. Nelson Mandela and Martin Luther King, Jr., were probably more free in jail than many other men who were never incarcerated. As Epictetus put it centuries ago, "He whose body is chained, and his soul unbound, is free."[19] Your mind is the only thing that you control in prison or jail. It is in your capacity to decide what to think or believe and whether to have a positive or negative attitude. Whether something enters your mind is up to you.

You also control your emotions. It is within your capacity to decide how you feel—whether to react with anger, fear, or hate—for example. What you feel is up to you. Nothing else is under your control. The property you acquired is not under your control in prison. No one in prison who owns gold necklaces and fine clothes can wear them. Their money, cars, and houses are beyond their reach.

You are under someone else's control. Your body is guarded day and night—24-7. You are told when to go or come, when to sleep, and when to eat. As long as you do what you are told, what you think or feel is of little concern to anybody in authority except when it gives evidence of a "bad attitude."

As your body is guarded, you must guard your mind, emotions, and spirit. This is done by avoiding negative thoughts, emotions, and evil in any form.

The ultimate control of your life rests not with state jailers and prison guards, but rather with you. You have the key. You can see the light of day long before you ever get out of prison if you use your mind for what your maker intended.

Overcome Your Past

A friend quotes a line from a baccalaureate address he heard over fifty years ago. The speaker said, "Don't let your handicaps handicap you." A prison record is a definite handicap, but it is not necessarily the end of your life—or the world. That is especially true if you do not internalize the values of your prison experience. I grew up on welfare in a single parent family. But, by the grace of God, welfare was not in me. Just because you were in prison is no reason for prison to be in you. Where you are going is far more important than where you have been. That assumes, heaven willing, that you are going in right direction.

You can never avoid the consequences of your criminal history, especially if it involved crimes of "moral turpitude." The law defines moral turpitude as "an act of baseness, vileness, or depravity in the private and social duties which a man owes to his fellow man or to society in general, contrary to the accepted and customary rule of rights and duty between man and man."[20] By this standard just about any low down thing a person does, especially if it involves dishonesty, regardless of whether it is a felony or misdemeanor, is likely to be considered moral turpitude. That means your past can be used to impeach you or show that you are not worthy of belief—and serve as a legitimate basis for discriminating against you in virtually every area of life. In a word, being "as nasty as you want to be" has consequences for a long time. What elementary school teachers told me years ago is still true: "Your record will follow you!"

5.3 MENTORING

Follow the Examples of Good Role Models

You may have to get your mentoring vicariously by reading books like this. All of us need someone like this who will dare to tell us the unvarnished truth. When we butt heads with someone whose point of view is different from our own, it is like "iron sharpening iron." This process cannot help but make you better. There is a good reason that athletes with "game" improve by playing or practicing against someone of equal or greater ability.

Role models are important in your rehabilitation. The value of role models is that they show us what is possible. Instead of looking up to them, "look into them" to figure out what made them successful. Let me commend Joseph to you (Genesis Chapters 37, 39-45 NKJV).

The Bible tells the story of Joseph who was a completely innocent young man. He was thrown in a pit by his brothers and sold into slavery. Through a false accusation he was eventually thrown in prison. But he did not become bitter. He used the spiritual gifts God gave him and he was faithful and trustworthy in every position he held. When he was finally elevated to the position of Prime Minister of Egypt, he looked back on his experience and concluded that:

> God had caused him to forget about the mistreatment he was forced to endure; and God made him fruitful and successful in a foreign land.

The relevance of this story for you is that only God can save you from the bitterness that so often affects people who spend time in prison, especially through no fault of their own. Let God transform your attitude and life. Instead of getting bitter, get better. Also, you can be successful anywhere if God is with you. Success is not always found in ideal circumstances where everything one needs is at hand. Further, you do not have to go to another city or have another relationship to make it. You can do it by "letting your bucket down where you are." In other words, there are opportunities to begin over—right where you are.

If the life of Joseph inspired you, it is possible that your life will become a contemporary model for someone else! That is especially true for those who have been exonerated after a wrongful conviction.

As helpful as good role models can be, the model you choose to get your life back on track will need to be developed based upon the unique circumstances that you face. What worked for somebody else may not work for you. Like a suit of clothes, the plan you devise for the next phase of your life will have to be tailored to fit you. This has been confirmed by studies, which show that in business it is a mistake to try to do what other successful people have done because what worked for them in their situation may not make sense for anyone else. What is of more benefit is focusing on how "great leaders think." In a word, they tend to be "integrative" thinkers, which mean taking competing ideas and developing a new one that is better than either by itself.[21]

5.4 DISCIPLINE [SELF-CONTROL]

Wait For What You Want

The ability to delay gratification and resist one's impulses has been identified as a psychological skill of great importance because it is the basis of all "emotional self control." The reason is that "all emotions, by their very name, lead to one or another impulse to act."[22]

These principles were illustrated by the "marshmallow test" which came from an experiment at Stanford University. The experimenter told a group of four year olds if they waited until he ran an errand they could have two marshmallows for a snack. But if they did not wait until then, they could have only one and they could have it immediately.

The experimenter was gone fifteen to twenty minutes. In order to deal with their struggle to wait for two marshmallows, some of the children "covered their eyes so they wouldn't have to stare at the temptation, or rested their heads in their arms, talked to themselves, sung, played games with their hands and feet, even tried to go to sleep." These kindergartners got the two marshmallows. But the others grabbed the one marshmallow within seconds of the experimenter's departure from the room.[23]

Twelve to fourteen years later, the children who were able to wait for the second marshmallow were shown to have been much more successful and better able to cope with life's problems than those who could not restrain themselves and quickly ate their one marshmallow. The former were better students, and had higher SAT test scores, and showed less delinquency associated with poor impulse control than the latter.[24]

This experiment clearly shows the reward and benefits of the ability to "delay gratification in pursuit of goals."[25] That is why Daniel Goleman calls impulse control "the master aptitude." It is nothing less than becoming your own boss!

The implications of this study for you are of great significance. Mastering the ability to delay gratification will serve you well not only behind bars, but also when you are released. There will be lots of things you want that you will not have the money to buy immediately. Learning to wait until you have saved the money to buy them is a far better option than resorting to crime or credit to get them. Learn how to wait for what you want! Do not assume that waiting means that there is nothing for you to do in the meantime—successful people work while they wait.

Don't Make the Same Mistake Twice

A recidivist is a person who was too dumb to learn from his or her mistakes or too smart for his or her own good. A little knowledge is often a dangerous thing. It can lead one to think more highly of himself or herself than he or she should. Pride always goes before a fall.

Do not give yourself so much credit for smarts that you think your time behind bars has put you in a better position to commit the perfect crime. The temptation may be to think, "Next time I'll do it right." Forget about it! That is recidivist thinking that will get you back in trouble.

There are people behind bars with advanced degrees—Masters, Ph.D.s, medical, dental, and law. What makes you think you are so smart that you will avoid their fate? In matching wits with "the man," you lost the last time, and guess what? You will lose again—and again. But not just you, but also your family!

The smartest criminals eventually get caught. They learn that crime does not pay. Now that you have had a taste of jail or prison, the evidence that you were not as smart as you thought you were and that you have learned from your mistakes is a commitment to go straight and "keep your nose clean." Which animals do you think are the smartest, the ones in a zoo or those that are still in the wild?

If you are one of the people who were wrongly convicted, you have every right to insist on your innocence. But in the absence of DNA evidence or a recanting witness, you may have to live with the consequences of the failure of an imperfect system of justice.

If you continue to insist on your innocence it will probably be interpreted to mean that you have not accepted responsibility for your crimes and have not been rehabilitated. On the other hand, if you admit to yourself and others that you are guilty of an offense you did not commit, you are likely to pay a high psychological price for it.

Regardless of your circumstances, the Serenity Prayer contains timeless wisdom that speaks to you. Seek the "serenity to accept the things that you cannot change, the courage to change the things you can and the wisdom to know the difference." You can not change the system—the prison, law enforcement officers, probation/parole officers, or judges. You can change yourself, your attitude and thoughts. As behavior follows thoughts and beliefs, coming to terms with this is a critically important step on your journey toward wholeness.

Get Yourself a Governor

Some machines have governors. They keep them from going too fast, regardless of who the operator is. As human beings, we also have governors. They are our mind and conscience. They tell us how fast to go. Unfortunately the governors with which we were born wear out or become dysfunctional from misuse or lack of use. These internal controls have to be repaired. But even in those whose internal controls work properly, there is a need for a governor. For persons of faith, the governor is the presence of the Holy Spirit who makes us behave by regulating our speech and conduct. He is available to all who accept a relationship with Jesus Christ, God's son. Living wide open is a prescription for disaster.

Be Nice, Especially When It Does Not Cost You Anything

It is true that a little niceness goes a long ways and it is false that "nice guys finish last." You can not afford to be nice if it is going to cost you your freedom. Get used to saying no and meaning it, even when you are being nice.

The notion of self-discipline means that you make yourself do what needs to be done. No one else can do it nearly as well as you can do it. But, in doing what you need to do, there is no need or benefit in being rude to people. One never knows when the people who were "dissed" will be needed.

Ask for What You Want

The Bible is right: "You have not because you ask not." That is true of God and everybody else. The culture says demand what you want and be assertive in doing it. But people are much more likely to respond to you in a favorable way if you ask in a nice way and say please.

Do you want a job, raise, or promotion? Ask for it. The problem with too many people is that they do not ask enough of themselves or life. The better you prepare yourself for life the more you can demand of others—and life. Why should you get what you want when others are standing in line for it, too? You must realize that everything in life that is worth having, somebody else wants it, too. When life asks you why you should receive what you ask for, be prepared to give a good answer. One thing is certain, life does not reward indolence, wickedness, ignorance, or criminal conduct.

Forget Trying to Be Slick

You are not in a position to demand anything from anybody. The price of "screwing up" is that people are not going to readily accept or forgive you. The most you can expect is a reasonable chance to prove yourself. But to be trusted to do right and become a responsible member of society will take time—and proof that you are a changed person. The burden is on you, not members of your family, employers or friends. The seductive argument that society has to prove that you are accepted is like the jury argument by some slick lawyers that a verdict should not be influenced by sympathy. What is the best way to prove that a verdict is not influenced by sympathy? It is to rule against or give an inadequate verdict to one's opponent. That sounds like an attempt to manipulate people. That is right up there with the line that young men use on gullible young women—"If you love me, prove it."

People who are wise to these tricks are not likely to fall for them. Trying to con them will just expose you for the person you still are—an exploiter who uses people to get what he wants through any means, including deception.

The Bible says: "Do not be deceived: Evil company corrupts good habits" (I Cor. 15:33 NKJV). No where is it truer than prison where one is constantly in bad company. If you want to successfully rehabilitate yourself, do not learn the anti-social attitudes and skills of the people you have been forced to associate with. One of the reasons employers and others are wary of having or wanting anything to do with someone with a prison record is the widespread belief that prison is a place for criminals to refine their ability to commit crimes rather than get rehabilitated. The best way to confound family members and friends is to avoid even the appearance of trying to be "slick." Whatever you learned about being "slick," you simply need to "forgeddah'bout it." All being slick will get you is a trip back to wherever you came from! The original "slick Willie" was Jacob, the biblical character. While he did not end up in jail, his bad character was replicated in his sons and he paid a high price for being a trickster in heartache and pain.

In every community there are tricksters who specialize in running con games that are played on the unsuspecting and gullible. The more unsuspecting a person is the more likely he or she is to fall for the "okey-doke." There is a good reason that wolves dress in sheep's clothing, and fishermen hide their hook when they present bait to fish!

This process is a problem for at least two people, the perpetrator and the victim. If you run scams on people, regardless of how slick you are, you will eventually be found out. When that happens, you will be sent back to prison if what you did violates the law, or the terms of your parole.

The consequences can be just as bad for the victim. If the object of your life is to deceive people, there will always be people who are gullible enough to fall for just about any scam. This observation was confirmed by P.T. Barnum who said, "There's a sucker born every minute."[26] There are other aphorisms which reflect this truth:

"A fool and his money are soon parted."[27]
"A fool believes everything."[28]
"There is no fool like an old fool."[29]

The "convict code" discourages inmates from being suckers. But it is arguable that in doing things that got you locked up, that is what you have become—a sucker.

The method of choice by con artists of every generation is the lie, which by definition is a falsehood that is told for the purpose of deceiving someone. The worst liars are pathological. According to scholars, there are three kinds of pathological liars:

In hysterical lying, the "liar believes the lie;"

In sociopathic lying, the object of the liar is to "deceive for personal gain without a sense of guilt;" and

In mythomanical lying, the "liar makes up a complicated story that he tries to convince others to believe."[30]

Nothing short of a powerful religious experience that radically alters a person's life can permanently cure pathological lying. If nothing else, the above categories might offer insight into why you act the way you act.

The words of Walter Scott, which were made famous by their use by the late Senator Sam Irvin during various hearings on the Watergate conspiracy that resulted in the imprisonment of several members of the Nixon Administration and the disgrace of President Richard Nixon, are still true:

Oh what a tangled web we weave,
When first we practice to deceive.[31]

Watch Your Mouth

If you don't tell people you are an ex-inmate they will never know. In the circles you need to move in to be successful now, a prison record is not going to improve your "creds." In fact, it is likely to be counterproductive. Forget the street talk, profanity, and prison lingo, and get a socially acceptable vocabulary. The only time it is advisable to talk about your past is when you are asked on an application for a job—or when you talk to your pastor or priest. It goes without saying that you must always tell the truth in your new life. Lying about your past can cause you far more problems than it is worth. If you get a job by lying, you will be fired when it is discovered. Moreover, you will create a psychological prison for yourself through fear of being found out.

If you do not tell people what is going on with you or act it out, they will never know. Why do you feel a need to talk about your past to total strangers? What works in hip-hop culture is likely to back fire on you in the real world which does not operate on the basis of prison culture in values, speech, or dress.

Few people will feel sorry for you because you say, "I used to be on the streets." Their answer is likely to be, "So?" The same reaction is likely to come when you say, "I did time in prison." Some may say, "It sounds like a personal problem to me"—and slam the door of opportunity you are trying to enter in your face. As a man told me, "When you tell people your business, half of the people don't care, the other half are glad of it."

The simple truth is that people who are insecure tend to talk too much. If there are things you need to confess, do not tell them to casual associates or people you may work with. Telling the members of your family is not always a good idea. You can always tell God. Find a minister, priest, or counselor. They will not judge you or hold what you say against you and, unless you tell them you plan to kill somebody, will not tell anybody else.

Another side of this issue is that you cannot say whatever you want to say and stay employed or on good terms with other people you need. "Bite your tongue," as they say. One of the most painful things we have to do is listen sometimes to things we do not want to hear without responding inappropriately because what we say can hurt us or keep us from reaching our goals.

Become A Self-Starter

Nobody will tell you when to go or come. It is up to you. Nobody is going to be there to wake you up to get to work on time or tell you when to go to bed. You have to be a self-starter. The motivation to succeed has to come from within you. Employers will quickly get tired of the lame excuse that you "overslept."

Nothing worthwhile will fall in your lap. You cannot depend on luck. The harder you work the luckier you will get. You have to get up early to seek it. The early bird gets the worm. No employer is going to be impressed with a job seeker who shows up at eleven o'clock to make an application.

Realize That The Night Time is Not Always the Right Time

Go home at a reasonable time. The terms of your parole or probation may include this condition in the form of a curfew. If not, it is a good strategy for staying out of trouble. Nothing good happens in the streets at night. Anything worth doing can be done before a late hour at night. The Bible is right: "Men loved darkness rather than light, because their deeds were evil" (St. John 3:19 NKJV). The only time the night time is the right time is when it is necessary for you to be at work, go to school or do something else that is constructive.

People who hang out late at night are often associated with crime. One of the best strategies you can use to stay out of trouble is going home at a reasonable time. There is nothing to be gained from "running the streets," anytime—day or night—except trouble.

5.5 MOTIVATION

Get and Stay Motivated

One of the best sources of instruction I have ever read on motivation is in the book of Nehemiah in the Bible. Nehemiah teaches us that the way to motivate people is to meet their needs. The people he motivated had two major needs: security and self-esteem. Their needs were related to the destruction of the walls of their city. When they were shown how to get their needs met, the work of completing the rebuilding of the walls was accomplished in short order. They worked hard because they saw that there was something in it for them. Many of us will work hard for someone else's benefit out of a sense of altruism. But the success of capitalism in transforming the world and lifting millions of people out of poverty bears witness to the power that people have when they act on their enlightened self-interest. The people who are most successful in business or any other area of life find needs and meet them.

Abraham Maslow talks about motivation in terms of a hierarchy of needs. In a sense, what he says is virtually the same thing Nehemiah discovered: People are motivated when their needs are met.

Guess who stands to gain the most from dealing with the needs in your life? You need security and self-esteem like everybody else. Given the needs that you have right now, no one should have to motivate you. If what you have been deprived of by your choices and the way you are regarded by society—and even members of your family—are not enough to make you want to do better, you have a lot more work to do on yourself. No one can do it but you! Many correctional institutions have various behavior modification programs in place. But they will not work for you unless you are motivated to change yourself. I submit that it is only when you discover the benefit in rehabilitation strategies for you and not the prison, that they motivate you to cooperate with those who are trying to help you. A good result is not likely to be achieved through manipulation or coercion. It is easy for people to play the game just to get out of a bind with no lasting effect on their behavior.

It is not too late to make your life count. Go for it!

Play Catch Up

In the days of segregation, some black school teachers told black students, "You are behind, and you are going to have to run twice as fast to catch up." That is as true of the race of life as it is of education. But it can be done!

Whatever amount of time you wasted before your behavior got you in trouble and you were out of circulation in jail or prison is the ground you have to make up, and now cover. If you use your time wisely while you are incarcerated, the ground you will have to cover will not be nearly as great as it will be if you waste your time being bitter, angry, or doing something else that is negative. That is why I contend that rehabilitation begins long before a prisoner's release. It has to start at the time the jury returns a guilty verdict. In fact, the time of arrest is not too soon.

Beware of Complacency

Being in trouble should have served as a wake-up call. How you respond to this circumstance determines whether the message was heard. If you are satisfied with your life as it is, nothing will change when you get out of prison. Wanting to do better or be better is a good sign that you are headed in the right direction.

Work on Your Game

How many times have you seen kids working on their game? Hour after hour on hot asphalt basketball courts, they practice their shots; they learn to dribble with both hands in order to execute their moves and avoid defenders. They were not born doing what they learned to do. They get "game" by working on their skills. You can do the same thing. This includes reading, expanding your vocabulary, improving your manners, straightening out your morals, consistently doing what is right, working on broken relationships, respecting the property of others, and becoming self-sufficient without abusing, exploiting, or taking advantage of others. When you do these basic things, voila, people will see that you, too, have game in the most important contest of all—life!

What is ironic is that many of you think you are tough. If you are as tough as you think you are, why not prove it by standing up to yourself and saying no to the impulse to do what is wrong? Is the tough look and talk just a façade for inner insecurity? Throughout this book I have emphasized the need for self-discipline. All that involves is the ability to master yourself. Solomon, reputed to be the wisest man to ever live, said, "He who is slow to anger is better than the mighty, and he who rules his spirit than he who takes a city" (Proverbs 16:32 NKJV).

Here is another question: Why are you letting people who do not care about you or anything else except "bling," dictate what you believe or define what is acceptable behavior? You are free. Letting someone impose their values on you violates your right of self-determination and makes you their slave. If you let that happen, you are as much in bondage outside as you were when you were in prison.

Remake Yourself

When a person messes up his or her life, it can only be changed through rebirth. A minister tells a story about a young man with character issues. When reproached, he excused himself by saying, "I was born this way." To this, the minister replied, "That is why you need to be born again." This is a choice that allows a person's character to be repaired.

Recognizing that change must occur from the inside out, some or all of the following are required:

(a) Begin by straightening out "stinking thinking." You can't drive a bent nail—not straight anyway. It has to be straightened out first.
(b) Replace your value system.
(c) Re-build your self-esteem by thinking positive thoughts and doing good works.
(d) Exchange a negative attitude with a positive attitude.
(e) Acquire respect for authority.
(f) Assume responsibility. (Don't blame others for your screw up)
(g) Allow God to heal the memories of your past (malparenting, abuse, etc).
(h) Accept accountability to:
    1. Self
    2. Others
    3. State
    4. God
(I) Clarify your identity.
(j) Overcome fear of failure.
(k) Keep fear of criticism and the need for approval in bounds.

After all you have been through, if you still need someone to motivate you to do right, avoid trouble in the future, and improve yourself, there is something seriously wrong with you. First of all, nobody can motivate you but you. If you are not motivated to help yourself and take advantage of programs offered by the state to rehabilitate you, your choices of succeeding on the outside are slim. Some institutions make participation in such programs mandatory. I doubt that this is a good idea because as Samuel Butler said: "He that complies against his will is of his opinion still." Besides, it is still true that "you can lead a horse to the water but you cannot make him drink." It is only when he gets thirsty enough he will drink on his own. That is reminiscent of the conventional thinking about alcoholism and other addictions—it is only when the person hits rock bottom that there is any real hope for him or her.

5.6 RESPECT/MANNERS

Respect Yourself and Others

If you want respect, give it. What you give comes back to you. The Bible is right: "For whatever a man sows, that he will also reap" (Gal. 6:7 NKJV). You cannot plant collards and get cauliflower.

There ought to be some things that you will not do because you have too high a regard for yourself. People with low self-esteem do "low down" things! The best way to feel good about yourself and get other people to treat you better is stop doing things that make you look bad, feel bad or cause others to treat you that way. This may be as simple as improving your manners or etiquette. There is a relationship between manners and morals. If you respect yourself and others, you will get respect. Why should anyone respect you if you do not respect yourself?

Do not get bent out of shape over real or imagined slights. Getting "dissed" is nothing to go back to jail for. Besides, when you respect yourself, it becomes easy to just walk away. The better you feel about yourself, the less of a problem this becomes. If you have low self-esteem, are not sure of who you are as a person, and have a chip on your shoulder, you are susceptible to all kinds of negative behavior, including fighting and violence in other forms. Haven't you heard, "Sticks and stones may break my bones, but words will never harm me?"

Have you seen people who got fighting mad because they thought someone had "dissed" them? Instead of getting mad, a better strategy is to use what people say to get better. Consider first whether it is true. If it is, change in response to it. If it is not, ignore it. Sometimes it is just a matter of the person who offended you having bad manners instead of an intent to harm you—or motivation by racism.

Too much time is spent on the issue of low self-esteem. The easiest way to get over that problem is stop doing things that make you feel badly about yourself. Do good deeds instead of bad deeds, and, voila, you will feel good about yourself. When you feel good about yourself, you cannot help but have self respect. This is an act of self-affirmation and empowerment. If you feel badly about the things you have done, it is a sign that you are not as far gone as you and others may think.

Respect for authority is a big issue for people behind bars. There, you do not have any choice. But it is a good idea for you when you are released because you will deal with police officers in the community and other authority figures on the job and the place you live. That is true of everybody. Why do you think you do not have to do it?

CHAPTER SIX
The People in Your Life

Everything worthwhile in life is accomplished through people. That is true of business and virtually every other area of interest.

At a personal level, we are shaped for good or ill by the people in our lives. That is true whether they are relatives or just friends. Their potential to hurt or help us is the result of their closeness to us. Our enemies cannot exert the same influence on us because we keep them at arm's length. This point is illustrated by the anecdote that is told about the administration of President Warren G. Harding, which was notoriously corrupt. When someone told the President that he needed to watch his enemies, he reportedly said, "It is not my enemies who are causing my problems but rather my d— friends."[1] The purpose of this chapter is to offer suggestions to help you deal with the people in your life, regardless of whether they are family or friends.

6.1 FRIENDS

Don't Let Anybody Pull Your Strings

Forget the ghetto ethic by which you have lived. All it ever got you was pain, prison and poverty. There are times when being a responsible citizen of your community requires your cooperation in getting folk like you used to be off the streets. That means if you are where a crime is committed, cooperation with the police is what you have to do.

Snitching is portrayed as the worst thing one can do because it destroys his or her "creds." What it boils down to is what kind of community you want to live and raise your family in. There are some things worse than death and one is living in fear of death.

There is no substitute for not letting what others say or do cause you to lose control of yourself. Howard Thurman, in *Jesus and the Disinherited*, addressed this issue in the following terms:

"Anyone who permits another to determine the quality of his inner life gives into the hands of the other the keys to his destiny. If a man knows precisely what he can do to you or what epithet he can hold against you in order to make you lose your temper, your equilibrium, then, he can always keep you under subjection. It is a man's reaction to things that determines their ability to exercise power over him."[2]

Watch the Folk You Associate With

In prison you did not have any choice in the matter of whom you associated with. Now you do. Some will say you think you are better than they are if you avoid the "wrong crowd." Many people believe "birds of feather flock together." So they say they are your friends? Do not allow your fresh start to be crippled by other folk's bad habits—and reputations. Many folk end up in jail because they were in the wrong place at the wrong time with so-called friends. They were with "the wrong crowd." Drugs or other contraband that belong to someone else may be "pinned" on you. That could mean a trip before a judge and return to jail or prison. What the Bible say is still true: "Bad company corrupts good morals" (1 Cor.15:33 KJV).

Do Not Think Your Friends Will Be Eager to Assist You

I have offered for political office, and I know from first hand experience that people you think are your friends may not be eager to help you. In fact, some will not return your telephone calls or respond to your letters. Some do not feel comfortable telling you they will not support you or that they think your opponent is a better candidate. They just ignore you—and avoid you like the proverbial plague. Some treated me this way after telling me they would support me. I discovered that some were in my opponent's camp.

Do not be surprised if something like that happens to you when you get out of prison. If you do not believe me, go ahead and write them any way. But if they do not respond to your letter, do not waste your time calling them—and for God's sake, do not just show up on their door steps. Keep some semblance of pride and do not grovel to be with or get the help of people who have moved on and, for whatever reason, do not want to be bothered with you.

The late Pearly Brown, a street preacher, used to sing a song that included this line: "Don't take everybody to be your friend." That was good advice then, and it is still good advice.

Sometimes it is a mistake to take everyone to be your friend, under the best of circumstances, but especially for someone in your position. More often than not, the people you think are your friends will cause you to get in trouble. It happens in subtle ways. For example, a person you barely know may ask you to do him a favor such as carrying a package out of a store. If it contains merchandise that was not paid for, and you are caught, you just got a ticket back to jail.

Something similar occurs when a person who claims to be your friend asks you for a ride in your car or gives you a ride in his car and drugs are found after a police stop. Several of my former clients who got arrested under these circumstances said, "The stuff was not mine, and the driver will testify to that."

I always replied, "Want to bet?" Of course they never do.

Believe it or not, there are people who ask people they call friends to open bank accounts for them or make deposits into accounts that are already set up. Obviously, there is no limit to the ways people can misuse their so-called friends.

Friends do not get each other into trouble. Anybody who does that is not your friend. The best policy is to not associate with people who do not care about you.

Avoid People Who Have Nothing to Lose

One of my friends who had enjoyed great success in his profession after growing up in a housing project got into trouble. He raises the issue of proportionality in sentencing. His point is that as a professional person he paid a higher price for his crime than an "ordinary" criminal because he not only did time, but also lost his license to practice his profession and paid a fine.

While it is easy to dismiss this position as the product of arrogance, and a lack of contrition, the point that it illustrates deserves serious consideration by every person who contemplates committing a criminal act, but especially those who have a lot to lose. The point is that the person who has the most to lose will always pay the highest price for his misdeeds. That is why a person with a lot to lose should be wary of any thing or relationship that might place it at risk.

In theory, the legal system is not supposed to cut a person any "slack" because of who he or she is. Sometimes it is just the opposite as we saw in the cases of Paris Hilton, Nicole Richie, Martha Stewart, and most recently, Michael Vick. In their cases, celebrity was a definite disadvantage. The average person who is accustomed to seeing big shots get away with murder probably gets a perverse sense of satisfaction out of the downfalls of folk who think or are treated as if they are better than everyone else.

Ironically, people with a lot to lose often associate with people who may be beneath them morally and socially in order to avoid giving the impression that they think they are too good to associate with the people they grew up with, and often include them in their entourages. That you do this may be as much an indication of what kind of person you are as it is the kind of folk you are comfortable around. It is, after all, possible to want something out of life without thinking or acting as if you are better than anyone else. Sometimes, insecure people of means hang out with unsavory and under-educated folk because they like being "brown nosed" by people who say what they want to hear.

One of the big issues people with money should ponder in their time in prison is what is it about themselves that made them need to be surrounded by sycophants, cronies and yes men from "the hood." Was it a sense of inferiority or low self-esteem that was made bearable by being around someone worse off? What's up with the juvenile, sophomoric tendency to form circles of "groupies" who are paid for friendship with the perquisites of your success? Other issues to ponder are what makes you think you can trust so-called friends to look out for your interest who have not done that for themselves and why you have a need to be the center of their attention. These issues need to be explored and addressed with the assistance of someone who will tell you the unvarnished truth, whether you want to hear it or not. In fact, until you are ready for that, you are probably not ready for release or a resumption of your career. This is just the beginning. The hardest work remains to be done on your character. That involves a change in values and an understanding of the limits of loyalty, the meaning of citizenship, and acceptance of responsibility for personal behavior.

While any blemish on the name of a person whose livelihood depends upon the favor of the public is costly, there are entertainers and athletes who have been involved in drugs, been prosecuted for violent assaults, committed sexual offenses, accused of murder, convicted of driving while under the influence of alcohol, gamed the stock market, associated with gambling activities that did not involve their sport, given obscene gestures to fans, said intolerant things about gay people, and made hateful remarks about Jews, African Americans, and immigrants of various nationalities. Many of the worst offenders paid dearly for their indiscretions and were allowed to resume their careers with very little evidence that they were rehabilitated and sometimes without so much as an apology to the people who were hurt or offended. About the only people who are permanently consigned to the status of persona non grata are the ones who bet on the team they are playing for or managing. By the standard that has been applied to others, there is no reason why, if you take seriously the need to change your life and behavior, you cannot be redeemed.

Whether you are restored depends upon your attitude. If you get out of prison feeling bitter or seeking revenge, your life will never resume its upward trajectory. Rather it will continue its downward spiral.

Politicians, entertainers, and athletes who have always had others looking up to them probably cannot remember a time when their celebrity did not get them all kinds of benefits that they were not entitled to on the basis of their character—or merit. It is ironic that all of the special attention and favoritism do not satisfy the underlying need for approval and affirmation that makes athletes hang out with people who make them feel good about themselves. Money and the things money can buy can not change what we think about ourselves. A person of bad character with a lot of money, regardless of how it was obtained, is still the same person. We have seen the effects of sudden wealth on people who have won the lottery. Many of them end up broke and sometimes in trouble within a short period of time.

If you learn something from your experience that makes you realize that you are no better than anyone else and resolve that from this point forward you will live in accordance with the standards of behavior that govern the behavior of everybody else, then you are well on the way towards rehabilitation.

Just treating a person as if he or she is special is not always enough to make him or her feel that way. If people do not have a sense of self-worth that is rooted in something more durable than the cheers of the crowd or the adulation of fans, what happened to Michael Vick can easily happen to any of the rest of us who succeed off the football field. Without a functioning moral compass to guide us, it is easy to get off course. But thankfully, it is possible to fix our compass and get back on the right track through a relationship with God—and the guidance of committed friends who love us enough to tell us the truth.

6.2 FAMILY

Deal with Your Family History

Who your father and mother were does not explain your situation. You are what you are because of choices you made. There are people who believe in a form of determinism that says that you can never rise above your background and that either your environment or genes determine your destiny. Do not believe it.

Too often, people who make mistakes are inclined to blame their family and their genes. While the "sins of the fathers" can be visited on their children, the choices you make are more likely to determine how your life turns out. This is another form of blaming.

There is no question that our family of origin can greatly influence us through the values we learn from them. But whether their demons are exorcized depends more on you than anybody else.

In my experience, the single biggest hang up which men in jail deal with is their reaction to the absence of their fathers. Ironically, they often replicate the problem by abandoning their own children. That is why one of the most important things you can do is rebuild your relationship with your family and children. Through this means you can break your family curse and exorcize your demons. I often tell couples in my counseling sessions that the best thing they can do for their children is let them see that you love each other. Their psychosexual development depends on your example—what you preach and practice.

Rebuild Your Support System

This means dealing with family issues. They should bear more responsibility for helping you then anyone else. But do not be surprised if people you hurt and whose good will you used up do not immediately rally to your side. With good reason, they are probably angry with you. Your spouse and children got along without you while you were away. Your children have not had you in their lives. Your wife or husband has had to be mother and father. The authority to manage the family and its financial affairs will not be quickly turned back over to you. Trust that was broken has to be earned all over again. That takes time. Be patient. When you show that you are not the same old person family members used to know, they will begin to treat you in a different way.

People in your church have a stake in this as well. If you hurt or embarrassed them, one of the first things you should do after setting your relationship right with family members is to go back to church, confess your sins, and ask for forgiveness and prayer. If you are not accepted and welcomed, find a church that will accept you. But do not think you will be allowed to work with the youth department or vulnerable young women. If you judge acceptance by the willingness of a church to give you unfettered access to its youth, you will not be accepted anywhere.

One impediment to finding acceptance in church is the threat that a person with a criminal record is thought to pose for other people. That is particularly true of people who committed sex crimes against children. Churches that have youth programs licensed by state agencies cannot have any person with a known felony conviction on its premises. Regular church ministries require fewer constraints, but a lot of vigilance. I know of a young man who visited his family's church for the mid-week prayer service and Bible study. Instead of going to an adult Bible class, he wanted to teach a children's class. What kind of suspicions do you think that aroused? When he was told no, he left and has not been back.

Don't Expect Too Much from Your Family

A person ought to always be able to go back home. But if that is the source of your problem, that may not always be a good idea. That is true of a bad neighborhood, a bad job, and yes—a bad family relationship.

The Israelites could not go back to Egypt. The Red Sea closed behind them (Ex.10:19 NKJV). Adam and Eve could not go back to the Garden of Eden because its entrance was guarded (Gen. 3:24 NKJV).

When people leave jobs they are often told, "Don't burn your bridges." Sometimes that depends on where they lead or where one is leaving. It is like the difference between playing linebacker or defensive back in football. Whereas a linebacker's first step is forward, a defensive back's first step is backward. Whether you go forward or backward, depends on the position you are in or the circumstances you face. There are times when a defensive back has to come up to stop a run and a linebacker has to drop back to defend against a pass.

According to Robert Frost, "Home is the place where, when you come there they have to let you in."[3] You may feel like somebody forgot to tell your family. The reality may be that where you used to live is no longer your home because your behavior has alienated the members of your family to the point that they feel no obligation to let you in when you get out of jail or prison. There are families that have been so abused by sons and daughters on drugs or with untreated mental health problems that they have just about disowned them. What Frost says is good poetry. But as an adult, your family does not have to "let you in," especially if you come back with the "s.o.s." that got you in trouble in the first place.

6.3 RELATIONSHIPS

Rebuild Broken Relationships

One of the first things that you should do is attempt to rebuild your relationships with people who love you that you have destroyed. Do not ask for anything except forgiveness. After you apologize sincerely, do not act like the cow that gave a bucket of milk and then kicked it over. That is done when you act apologetic one minute and then revert back to the behavioral pattern that ruined the relationship in the first place. If you used people, begged, borrowed without repaying, hurt people, lied, stole, or anything else, stop. That will do wonders to show that you are credible and deserving of a second chance. People do things to improve their "creds" on the street that get them into trouble. The focus on the outside needs to be on the things that will keep your "creds" in your family and community. If you do not receive forgiveness, move on—and do not become vindictive. Additional time for you to show you are sincere may be necessary for the people you have hurt to take another chance with you.

Stay Out of Toxic Relationships

Some people poison everything they come in contact with. You may be that kind of person. If so, you need to deal with that problem. What is it about yourself that alienates or antagonizes others? Discovering the answer to this question is an indispensable part of the process of rehabilitation.

What is it about you that causes everything you touch to come to nothing? Is it your addiction or just plain bad character? While you are ultimately responsible for the person you have become, it is undeniable that much of the incentive to be a toxic person is the result of a toxic culture. I believe it is possible to not only take a person out of the ghetto, but also the ghetto out of the person.

Stay Away From Toxic People

Some people are bad news. They poison every relationship they enter—and in the process taint or negatively impact everybody they come in contact with. There are folks who tear you down rather than build you up. They always have something up their sleeves. They are always scheming and scamming. Beware, lest you become just like them. Part of the point is illustrated by this scenario:

A man in a romantic relationship with a woman with whom he is "shacking" decides that he wants to end it for whatever reason and begins to pack his things to leave. Before he can leave, she blocks the door and one thing leads to another, and before he knows it, he strikes her.

Sometimes it is the woman who decides she no longer wants to be in a relationship that is not going anywhere or for some other reason. She asks the man to leave or tries to move out. In response, he stands in her way. In trying to leave, she strikes him and a fight ensues.

In either situation, the man is likely to be charged with "domestic violence." These cases are always taken seriously by policemen and the courts because they quickly escalate and spin out of control. When that happens, policemen are injured or killed, or one of the parties is injured or killed.

If I have seen these situations once, I have seen them dozens of times. In every instance, somebody ends up hurt—and someone ends up behind bars, usually the man. If you value your freedom, this is one more reason to be responsible in the relationships you enter or resume upon your release. If you were arrested for your inability to get along with someone before, what makes you think things will be any different this time? The best policy is to stay away from this kind of person.

If the person you were married to is in a new relationship or has moved on while you were in prison, do not succumb to the temptation to try to see her again. Stalking, making harassing telephone calls, or otherwise making a nuisance of yourself can cause you to be returned to prison. The absolute last thing you should do is threaten or attempt to physically hurt someone who has rejected you, regardless of what the person has done or said to you. Walk away! If the person does not want to be in a re-lationship with you, there is nothing you can do about it. Besides, when you feel good about yourself, you know that you can find new friends and romantic relationships.

6.4 PREPARE FOR RESTORATION

Ordinarily, when a crime is committed, it is considered to be against the state and not the individual or community. The theory of criminal justice known as restorative justice[4] is an alternative way of viewing the relationship between the offender, victim, and community. In either way of seeing this situation, the citizenship rights of the offender are taken away. But instead of treating crime as the exclusive province of the state, restorative justice privatizes it in the sense that it emphasizes the need for victim, offender, and their respective communities to seek ways to achieve reconcilia-tion and a renewed relationship. While the goal is to promote and protect the interests of all parties, the needs of victims are of paramount concern. This may involve some form of restitution which is designed to make the victim as close to whole as possible. It also demonstrates the desire of the offender to right a wrong and commitment to avoiding recidivism. Although restorative justice is important even when the victim is a total stranger, when it is considered that many crimes are committed against people who are related to the offender, a restorative justice approach has the potential to help put families back together. But whether it is an option for you depends upon the crime you committed, the sentence you received, the openness of the community to it, and the attitude of the victim. In some instances, some aspects of it may be included in the sentence along with jail or prison time. Of all the strategies for dealing with crime, restorative justice has the greatest potential to provide win-win solutions for everyone who is affected by a criminal act, because almost everyone who ends up in jail or prison eventually returns to his or her community of origin. If you get an opportunity to explore or experience restorative justice at any point, you should jump at it if you intend to do what is right by people you have hurt or disappointed. Think about it! This process may give you the possibility to not only get your family back, but also your citizenship rights. When you have messed up as badly as some of you have, it does not get any better than that!

Do not mistake this concept for "cheap grace." It is not. It takes a lot for a person to successfully go through the process of restoration. It involves, according to some scholars, at least four steps – confession, repentance, restitution, and reconciliation. If there has been no remorse for the wrong that was committed, it is highly unlikely that you will convince a court, parole board, or the people with whom you seek to be reconciled that you are serious about it. All that continuing to deny your guilt or blam-ing someone else for your problems will do is make you look like the same old person you have always been. Genuine sorrow for what you did will lead to acceptance of responsibility for your crime. That is why I contend that this is a spiritual matter and that it cannot be done by just making New Year's resolutions or promises to do better. It can only be done through God's help.

CHAPTER SEVEN
Getting What You Want the Right Way

Contemporary culture emphasizes "bling" and encourages people to get rich through any means necessary. In a word, that is a prescription for a long prison sentence or an early grave. If this is the price you have to pay for wealth, I hope you will realize that it costs too much before it is too late. As a capitalist and Christian, and let me say parenthetically that the two are not necessarily oxymoronic or incompatible, I believe there is nothing wrong with having things as long as they do not have you. The Bible talks a lot about money. It is all a matter of means—that is, how you get it. In this chapter, I suggest ways to get what you want out of life without paying for it with your freedom, dignity, or self-respect.

7.1 MONEY

Live within Your Means
(Translation: Do without what you do not have the money to buy.)

This is a hard lesson for folk who have never spent a day in jail or prison. Doing it requires discipline enough to say no to the hardest person in the world to say no to—yourself. That is true not just of money matters, but every other area of your life. The key to getting in control of your finances is a budget, which is a spending plan. You cannot spend more money than you have. If you cannot buy it with cash or fit the payments in your budget, you need to leave it alone. Clothes, cars, jewelry or other things do not "make the man." All they do is create a powerful incentive to resort to crime to get what you cannot afford. What Paul said long ago is still true: "The love of money is a root of all kinds of evil" (I Tim. 6:10 NKJV). I might add, and the things money can buy. It cannot buy love, self-respect, or high self-esteem. These must be acquired the old fashioned way. They have to be earned.

Use Credit as a Stepping Stone

Credit is not necessarily a bad thing. It depends on how it is used. It is an important means to an end by poor people who cannot afford to pay cash for a car or home. The sub-prime lending business is high risk because of the people who get their loans. But they serve a useful purpose in meeting the needs of high risk customers. You should beware of predatory lending practices. If you cannot pay a debt, do not make it. What was true in prison life is also true outside of prison—pay your debts. Violating this tenet of the "convict code" carries a severe penalty in prison.

Credit is an important step in rebuilding your life if you are faithful in paying debts. How you handle credit is a sign of what kind of character you have. If you do not pay your debts, people will think you have bad character—and with good reason. You promised to pay and didn't do what you said. Every time you make a promise, your integrity is on the line. There are bankers who will make loans on the basis of character—and the promise of the borrower to repay the loan. How much is your word worth?

Beware of Ill-Gotten Gain

Crime does not pay. It never has and never will. I do not know anyone who ultimately prospers from a life of crime or violating the rules of society, even when it is for the purpose of providing jobs for family members or so-called friends. In basketball, the athlete who scores by committing a foul is penalized. If he does it enough, he is put out of the game. Sometimes one flagrant foul is enough. But more importantly, not only is there a penalty, the athlete and his or her team are deprived of the points that result from a foul.

The same thing happens in football. If a lineman is caught holding, not only is the gain that results from it taken back, the team is also penalized. Something similar occurs in hockey. There is a penalty box for rule violators. There is no future in getting things in violation of the rules. Prosecutors and police officers have had the same experience in getting convictions for violations of the law. The penalty is that the tainted evidence and its fruits are excluded and convictions are overturned.

Moral: Whatever benefit is obtained through crime or not playing by the rules is taken away or is of only temporary benefit, if any.

One thing is certain; inmates do not drive Escalades in prison and do not wear "grilles," gold necklaces, or any other fruit of criminal conduct or trappings of a street lifestyle. Further, the government will take anything it can find, including cash, cars, land and homes that were associated with the criminal enterprise that resulted in your arrest and conviction.

This means that you have to play by the rules. If you live by the mantra of hip-hop culture, "wealth through any means necessary,"[1] it will not only cost you the money and things you acquire, but also your freedom—and possibly your life. Besides, there are a lot of things more important in life than "bling."

Make your own money and pay your own way—honestly. People will help you sometimes. But they will get tired of beggars, cheats, and liars. There is no substitute for obtaining your own money, the right way. As the song writer put it, "Mama may have, papa may have, but God bless the child who has his own."

7.2 WORK

Don't Be Too Proud to Work

Willingness to work hard will get you a long way. Being on time, showing up every day, and doing what you are told are critically important. All of these things are part of what is called work ethic. There is dignity in any honest hard work. If you cannot get the job you want, take the job you can get and work at it faithfully until a better opportunity comes along. Those who have, get. But those who do not have a job cannot seem to "catch a break." Employers are interested in those already gainfully employed who demonstrate minimal work skills and ethic. Do not think you are too good to work even a menial job if that is all you can find. Do not be like the man who refused a job that would have given him decent wages and a secure retirement because he said, "I can't let my women see me doing that."

Learn a Skilled Trade

A good job is still the best defense against poverty, powerlessness, and temptation that come from want. The best way to get it may be going to a trade school that is easily accessible through the network of vocational and adult education schools in most states. This may be the best investment you will ever make. When I was in high school, I took vocational courses. To this very day, hardly a week goes by that I do not use something I learned in those courses.

Learning a skill for which people will pay will pay dividends for the rest of your life. Booker T. Washington[2] was advocating this over a hundred years ago and what he thought is still ignored at our peril. Skilled trades are going begging because too many of this generation have not discovered the dignity of skilled labor. Interestingly, H. R. Russell, an Atlanta businessman, parlayed a trade as a plasterer into a multi-million dollar construction company. That can happen for you if you learn a trade and not just a few tricks of a trade.

Don't Expect Something for Nothing

Someone said you may not get everything you pay for, but you will certainly pay for everything you get. The moral is you do not get something for nothing. Everything worthwhile has a price tag on it.

Work for What You Want

If you cannot find the kind of job you want, take whatever honest job you can get. There is dignity in any kind of honest toil. Besides, if you have a job it is far easier to get another one than it is when you are unemployed. As my mother used to say, "Do not bother anything that does not belong to you. Anything worth having is worth working for."

Start a Business (legal, mind you!)

If all else fails, start your own business. You can behave so badly that few people will offer the kind of job that will allow you to make a living. All is not necessarily lost. Starting a business on a "shoe string" is the stuff of which legends are made in this land of incredible opportunity. But you must realize that running a legitimate business requires the same work ethic that is necessary to hold down a job—and far more discipline. Micro lending and micro economics offer viable options to entre- preneurs in third world countries. There is no reason why they will not work for you. Many people never explore the possibility of starting a small business because they mistakenly believe it takes a lot of money.

To succeed in business you have to be able to see an opportunity where others see obstacles. Thomas Edison said: "The reason opportunities are missed is that they show up dressed in overalls"[3] —they look like work that is too hard.

Do not succumb to the temptation to become a jailhouse racketeer by supplying items to your fellow inmates. If you have been smitten by the entrepreneurial bug, wait until you get out of prison to act on your business plans.

Work Hard and Smart

The harder you work and struggle, the luckier you will get. All looking for the easy way out will get you is—trouble. The harder you struggle, the more likely you will achieve success. Of course, this presupposes that you are also working smart. The story is told of a man who was engaged in a wood chopping contest. Every time his competitors looked around, he was sitting down. But at the end of the competition he had the biggest pile of wood. One of the contestants asked how he had won sitting down as much as he did. He answered, "When I was sitting down, I was sharpening my axe." Too many of you are working hard with a dull axe. If hard work alone was enough, many of our fathers would be rich because many of them worked hard all their lives. But in spite of the return on their labor, they kept their integrity.

Ordinarily, one does not have to be that much better than a competitor for a job to get it. But that changed when you got a prison record. Now you will have to be better to start and improve after that. It means you may have to start at a lower rung of the ladder; but if you climb, you can make it up the ladder.

Use Anti-Discrimination Laws

If all else fails, some of you may want to consider your legal options. Employers who refuse to hire you because you received a "less-than-honorable discharge" from the military may be in violation of laws which prohibit discrimination unless it can be shown that there is a relationship between your disqualification and job perfor- mance.[4]

In the case of credit requirements, as long as good credit is a business necessity of the job, employers can use it to disqualify applicants. Ordinarily, it cannot be used because of its "disparate impact on minorities."[5]

Use of arrest and criminal records in making employment decisions is also poten- tially violative of federal anti-discrimination laws because of its "disproportionate im- pact on blacks."[6] The only way an employer can require that successful applicants not have an arrest record is that it is shown to be necessary to the operation of the business. Similarly, when an employer refuses to hire you because you have been convicted of a crime, its conduct may be illegal if it cannot be established that the employer at least looked into the circumstances of your case and determined that hiring you would jeopardize the safe and efficient operation of the business.[7]

Some employers also have discriminatory grooming requirements. If they require men, for example, to have different hair styles from women there is at least a potential problem.[8] Although this is not as much of a problem as it used to be, it can still be a serious problem for black men who wear beards because the sensitivity of their skin to razors creates a serious health problem.

There is some law that holds that employers may not disqualify job applicants because their appearance is typical of members of a minority race.[9] What does that mean? Are baggy britches, braids, earrings, grills, and caps turned backwards or sideways typical of black people? Employers are probably going to get away with imposing dress requirements that are rationally related to their need for a safe and efficient work environment.

Let me ask you a question. Why would you go looking for a job looking like that? You have an absolute right to be an individual and flaunt your personal taste in appearance or dress. But you do not have a right to impose your dress standards on an employer. Since you need a job, it is incumbent on you to conform to reasonable appearance and dress standards.

As you can see, you have some rights under federal anti-discrimination laws. But by the time you get any benefit from using them to get a job, you will have starved. Filing a complaint with the Equal Employment Opportunity Commission is a relatively simple process, but it can take forever to produce results. Once filed and you are issued a right-to-sue letter, all that means is that you can file suit. Filing suits in federal court is an expensive, time-consuming process. As there are few lawyers who are willing to take on the cases of people who do not have a criminal record, try finding someone who will be willing to file suit for you in the hope he or she can convince a jury to give you some money for alleged discrimination against you because of your criminal history. Proceeding pro se may be your only option. But that should be done only in the most egregious cases. Federal courts, where most civil rights cases are filed, frown on pro se litigants who bring frivolous lawsuits. Your chances of convincing a jury to give you a monetary award are slim and none, if you survive attempts to get your case thrown out of court.

The chances are high that the employer will find someway of rationalizing its employment decision that makes a recovery difficult, if not impossible, even for litigants with good lawyers. Besides, getting a reputation for being "suit happy" may make it difficult to get any kind of job. The same prejudice is at work where unions are concerned. The perception of some businessmen is that African Americans are more likely to join or help organize a union than other workers. On paper, knowing and exercising your rights sounds good, but in the real world you cannot expect much practical benefit from the process. Another factor is the conservative swing of the courts. The law has been affected by the political climate and this makes it very hard to win any kind of employment discrimination case.

The best strategy is to present yourself as somebody who has some sense, and be appropriately dressed in accordance with conventional instead of ghetto standards. Remember, few people "get a second chance to make a good first impression."

If you are black, there are some things you cannot do anything about. One of them is discrimination. There are studies that show that white men with prison records receive more offers for an entry level job than black men with identical records and are offered jobs as often or more often than black men who have never been arrested.

The same standards which were used to assess the effect of race on job searches by ex-convicts found that black men who had never been in trouble with the law were about half as likely as white men with similar backgrounds to get a job offer. The black men whose job applications said they had spent time in prison were not as likely as white men with similar applications to get a job.[10]

For every ten white men without a conviction who got a job offer, more than seven white men with prison records received one. On the other hand, for every ten black men without a conviction, only about three with records were offered a job. This study of bias was based on data from New York City.[11] If you live in other parts of the country, the problem is probably much worse.

Develop A Good Work Ethic

Dr. Martin Luther King, Jr., observed that in the new age, black people would have to compete against people from all races for jobs. That is true of those who are leaving jail or prison. You will have to compete against people who do not have a record. To succeed you will have to work harder than your competitors.

Too many people enter trades or professions with no real commitment to practicing them with excellence. Dr. Martin Luther King, Jr., quoted a college president as saying: "A man should do his job so well that the living, the dead, and the unborn could do it no better."[12] The commitment to excellence even in performing a menial task was commended by Dr. King when he advised:

> If it falls your lot to be a street sweeper, sweep streets like Michelangelo painted pictures, like Shakespeare wrote poetry, like Beethoven composed music; sweep streets so well that all the host of Heaven and earth will have to pause and say, "Here lived a great street sweeper, who swept his job well."[13]

Play Hurt

The phrase "playing hurt" has a negative and positive connotation. The negative aspect of this phrase involves malingering. Malingering is a constant concern of employers because there are always people who, for whatever reason, exaggerate their symptoms for the purpose of avoiding work. Sometimes it is part of another form of fraud which involves pretending to be hurt in order to obtain workers' compensation or some other employment benefit. This is an area where character shows up in a way that may not be obvious to anyone but the management of the business. The positive side of playing hurt involves the mental toughness that is necessary to keep going in the face of adversity.

In order to help your employer or team you have to show up. Someone observed that "the greatest ability is availability." If you are not present, for all intents and purposes, you are not on the team. Every coach knows that regardless of how good a player is, he cannot score if he is not on the team. Regardless of how skilled you may be in doing your job, it does not mean anything if you do not regularly show up for work.

One of the things that separates a really good player from ordinary players is the ability to play while hurt. This requires toughness and the ability to tolerate pain. Depending on the nature of the injury, deciding to play while hurt may not always be a good idea. But with the usual nicks and scrapes that everybody gets in the game of life, you cannot expect people to give you a pass while you nurse your minor wounds. Lots of people do not always feel like getting up and going to work, but because they have responsibilities and obligations, they get up and go anyway. In assuming responsibility for your family, that is what you will have to do. In a word, going to work when you do not feel like it is the essence of what it means to "man up" to your responsibilities.

Many employers require that you report all injuries, regardless of how slight they may be. You have to make sure you comply with this requirement. If you have a serious injury and there is no light duty work, there may be times when you cannot work. But to stay in the good graces of your employer, your decision to not go to work must be supported by medical evidence.

7.3 VOCATIONAL OPTIONS

Realize That You Don't Have to Know Everything

You do not have to know everything in order to succeed. All you need to know is what you do not know. That takes real smarts. The reason is that you can always find a source of information for what you do not know. But without that much to start with, you can spend a lot of time going around in circles. Getting to this point requires you to be hard on yourself. As the poet said: "To thine own self be true." It is bad to believe a lie that you have been telling others about yourself. It is even worse to believe a lie you tell yourself.

Go To College

According to Napoleon Hill, "An educated person is one who knows how to acquire everything he needs in the attainment of his main purpose in life without violating the rights of his fellow men."[14] Getting to that point usually means going to college.

When I hear stories of the smarts of "jailhouse lawyers" that could put real lawyers to shame in drafting writs and other legal documents, I think what a waste of talent. But it may not be too late for them to put their abilities to better use in some other field.

It is never too late. You can start over. It may be that college is the only means to what will help you fulfill your life's purpose. So what that it is late in your life and you are far behind your contemporaries. It may have taken jail or prison to get you to realize that this is what you need to do. If that happened and you follow through and earn a high school diploma or a college degree, it may be that jail was one of the best things that ever happened to you. Caveat: There are some professions that will be off limits to you, and as a result you should thoroughly explore the requirements of any field you seek a degree in.

If you did not earn a college degree or some other credential that is necessary to get a good job, do not succumb to the temptation to falsify your resume by claiming credentials or expertise you do not have. This is done by many people who have never been to jail or prison. Consequently, employers are wary and most will check you out; if you lie about this matter and get caught, what have you gained? You are sure to be fired.

Prisons often have G.E.D. programs. If you do not have a high school diploma, get your G.E.D. You have to start somewhere. I know a person who went "from G.E.D. to Ph.D."[15]

Some colleges have degree programs that operate in prisons. This represents a significant change from what existed in the early 1990s when government funds financed college courses in hundreds of prisons. Those programs were opposed by victims' advocates and prison guards. When a "get-tough" environment was created in 1994, almost all federal funds were withdrawn from college programs behind bars.[16]

In the period since federal funding was cut off, the number of people in prison has almost doubled to 2.2 million and prison costs have increased over six fold to over $63 billion a year. These changes have caused a re-examination of research which proves that education is a "cost effective way of keeping ex-cons out of jail." According to a study of Texas prisoners, those who earn associates degree in prison have a recidivism rate of 27 percent compared with 43 percent for the state's total prison population.[17]

Get a Different Skill Set

Forget everything you learned in jail or prison about scamming, being tough, taking advantage of people, and doing things that are illegal or immoral.

Surviving outside of jail requires an entirely different skill set than the one which you acquired in "the joint"—and brought with you when you got incarcerated. Fighting, stealing, conniving, and taking what you want might have gotten good results on the streets and to some extent behind bars. But those things will get you a ticket back to where you came from.

The things you need to know now are how to use the language instead of people. Good language skills, written or verbal, will set you apart from your competitors for most jobs within your reach. Dressing for success is also important. But none of these things will matter if you do not have good work ethic, show up for whatever job you get, and give an honest day's work for whatever wages you agreed to accept.

If you learn a trade, have good work ethic, and are trustworthy, you are marketable. This will put you in the best possible position to be successful outside of prison. The best anti-recidivism strategy I can think of is a good marketable skill that is socially acceptable—i.e., "legit."

7.4 IMAGE

Put Your Best Foot Forward

If you do not tell anyone that you are an ex-inmate, except when asked on an employment application and other legal purposes, and do not act or look the part, no one will know. This places a premium on always putting your best foot forward.

Avoid conduct or attire that fits the stereotype of ex-prisoners. These include such things as braided hair, baggy clothes, and dreadlocks in some instances. A shaved head, tattoos on visible body parts, grills, earrings, and nose rings create a negative impression. These things are associated, in many folk's minds, with criminals.

If you do not have a tattoo anywhere on your body, do not get one. If you have one, get it removed. Why carry around such a visible, and to some, offensive reminder of your past? A tattoo sends the wrong message to potential employers. It's not about your rights. It is about presenting yourself to folk who have jobs and other benefits to offer you in a manner that will make them want to hire you.

Face it: Rightly or wrongly, people are already afraid of you. They may think you have AIDS or hepatitis C. Women may think you have been living "down low" because of reports of homosexual activity in prisons. Your race, combined with a prison record, and a threatening look makes your image worse and will contribute to your inability to get decent work or find new friends.

Before looking for a job, learn the secrets of "dressing for success" and acting like you are somebody with some sense who is going somewhere. If you do not clean up your thinking, it will be visible to every prospective employer through the way you dress or your hair style. Did you notice Michael Vick, the former Atlanta Falcons quarterback who got into trouble because of allegations that he was running a dog fighting ring, when he made his first appearance in court? He wore a coat and tie and was neatly groomed. While that is about making an impression on most potential jurors in federal court and the court of public opinion, it contains a valuable lesson for you that should be practiced when you go looking for a j.o.b.

The worst thing you can do is present yourself in a threatening or demanding manner. Nobody owes you anything. You had the same opportunity others had. All you have a right to expect is a chance—not a guarantee of success. Whether you get it depends more on you and your attitude than anyone else.

Only in the violent world of rap musicians is a prison record considered something to brag about and seen as something that is a "resume booster."[18] A record is used to improve their "street credibility"[19] even when the conviction is for something as serious as rape, armed robbery, or murder. But for everyone else who expects to earn a decent living, a prison record is a definite disadvantage that you will have to struggle to overcome for a long time, possibly the rest of your life.

7.5 FOCUS

Keep Your Eyes On the Ball

The Apostle Paul talked about this. He said of his work, "This one thing I do." (Phil. 3:13 KJV). Too many things on your plate will cause you to lose focus and become distracted. If you focus on yourself and what you can do to improve your life, you will get far better results than if you take a shotgun approach to life, which means focusing on too many things at a time.

CHAPTER EIGHT
Coping with Personal Problems

Life is beautiful and relatively simple and easy. Unfortunately, we make it ugly, hard and complex by the way we live. Regardless of how difficult one's life may become, dealing with stress by using drugs and alcohol will only exacerbate the underlying problem. Our creator made us with remarkable coping powers. It is possible to deal with what we go through with the natural and spiritual means he has provided. Sometimes all we need is help in discovering them.

The political reality today is that jails and prisons are being used as substitutes for the mental health facilities where people with serious mental disabilities were housed in the past. Many of these people do well as long as they take psychotropic medication. But once they are free, they often revert to their old pattern of behavior, which results in their re-arrest and incarceration.

Mental health problems are in a class by themselves in terms of the shame and pain they cause. But they often arise from or are exacerbated by the same conditions and choices that drive people to drink or use drugs. As these problems cannot be solved by a work of this kind, the best that can be hoped for is that persons who are laboring under a mental health disability will be encouraged to get the treatment they need to be able to function without becoming dependent or dangerous to themselves or others. They are discussed here in order to alert you to their potential effect on your effort to stay out of trouble.

By some accounts, as many as sixty percent of the people who are behind bars are there for a drug-related offense. This gives you and society a powerful incentive to address this issue.

8.1 DRUGS AND ALCOHOL

Get Help for Substance Abuse

If you don't smoke, drink or do drugs, don't start. If you have a problem with these or other behaviors, you need to get some help. Do not be too proud to get it. Most communities have mental health counselors who provide help with substance abuse and mental health problems. Group therapy may be invaluable.

Another alternative is joining AA—or some other twelve-step or self-help program. Joining a support group is another option. A good place to look for this option is the church you attend. In fact, this should be one of the factors you should consider in deciding which church to become involved in.

People respond to their problems in different ways. Some turn to drugs or alcohol in an effort to escape. When their problems cause pain, many people deal with it in the same way and for the same reason normal people handle a headache—to relieve or stop the pain. The difference is that in resorting to drugs and alcohol to self-medicate, they run the risk of becoming an addict or alcoholic. I heard a wise, old recovering alcoholic say, "It is not alcohol or drugs that is the problem." Rather, "Long before becoming physically addicted, whatever transforms them into addicts or alcoholics had begun to take root in their minds." That is why it is important for alcoholics and addicts to work on their minds as part of their recovery program.

Exorcizing one's demons is never easy. Mental health issues are hard to deal with. But drugs and alcohol present two of the greatest challenges one can face. They are probably more responsible for bad behavior than any other causes. However, they do not excuse it. Gambling, sexual addiction, and other compulsive conditions are also behind the spike in crime that is seen across this country. By some estimates, as many as sixty percent of the people who are in prison are there for drug related offenses.[1]

Others, as Stanton E. Samenow suggests, use drugs and alcohol as excuses for their criminal careers. I agree with his contention that the problem with the disease concept of alcoholism and drug addiction is that it relieves alcoholics and addicts of responsibility for their problems and too often allows it to become a socially acceptable excuse for bad behavior and criminal conduct.

What was said about denial and acceptance of responsibility are perhaps more apparent in the area of substance abuse than in the context of mental health. I approach these issues from the point of view that the disease concept makes sense of these conditions—both for the person who is addicted to drugs or alcohol and those who are trying to provide help in overcoming these conditions.

You can not pray your way out of a drug habit or alcohol problem. God will not do for you what you can do for yourself. One of my friends who admitted being an alcoholic said he is praying that God will take the taste of liquor out of his mouth. I told him I didn't think God was going to do it because he had the choice to drink or not drink and that he can quit anytime he decides to do it. This is another one of those instances that illustrates the difference between ability to do something and willingness to do it. It is a case of won't, not a matter of can't.

If you are not motivated to quit, nothing anyone says will make a difference. For most people, wanting to quit is the result of "hitting rock bottom." Some say things cannot get any worse than this. But they can. The late William Hutchings used to say: "Nothing is ever so bad it can't get worse or so good that it can't get better."

Cut Yourself a Little Slack

In your eagerness to convince people that you are a changed man or woman, do not promise more than you are capable of. I have heard people say, "I ain't ever going to drink no more of that rot gut liquor." The person who says that will probably be drunk again—sooner or later. The people who do the best are those who say, "By the help of God, I will not drink again" —or "I do not know what I will be doing tomorrow, but I will not drink today." These are folks who deal with alcoholism one day at a time. Relapse is an ever present possibility for any alcoholic or addict. But if a person learns from it, he or she may learn something about the nature of the disease that will ultimately help him or her overcome it. In this area, as in so many others, failure is not final. Just because you mess up does not mean that you will never be able to overcome your problem. That is why you and the people who love you should get some help. Investigate Alcoholics Anonymous, and related programs for drug addiction.

8.2 MENTAL HEALTH

The disease concept should make people more understanding of the plight of alcoholics and addicts. But instead of treating the disease, we have criminalized it. A prison experience is likely to produce loneliness, depression, anger, desperation, delusions, immorality, shame, guilt, and conflict. Some of these symptoms are probably normal and to be expected, especially depression. In the case of depression, Scott Peck[2] says, it may be beneficial. As conflict may signal a need for change in some area of life, depression may be an internal indication that something is wrong in the way we think or behave. The same can be said of the existential guilt and shame that are felt when one engages in bad behavior. That you are still capable of having these reactions is positive in the sense that they suggest that you may not be as far gone as some may think if you respond to them by changing the behavior that leads to these feelings or symptoms.

Deal with Mental Health Issues

A 2006 study by the United States Justice Department found that "56 percent of state prisoners, 45 percent of federal prisoners, and 64 percent of local jails' inmates suffer from mental illness." The same study found that there are more people with serious mental illnesses in state prisons than in state mental hospitals. When it is considered that this population has a high rate of suicide[3] and is responsible for an increased risk of homicides and other kinds of violence, the choice is either get the treatment you need or be subjected to involuntary treatment.

The tip-off that you may have a mental health issue could be as obvious as a tendency to blame everybody else but yourself for your problems or accepting too much responsibility. The former evidences an anti-social personality, and the latter is indicative of a neurotic condition. Acceptance of responsibility is generally a good indication of good mental health. But blaming is almost always a bad sign. It boils down to whether you can tell yourself the truth and say, for example, "I am in this mess because of decisions that I made." The moral of this is that both denial and blaming should be avoided. Scott Peck makes a helpful distinction between a person who is neurotic and one who has anti-social personally disorder. The neurotic takes too much responsibility by saying, "It's all my fault." On the other hand, the person with the anti-social personality disorder does not accept any responsibility. He says it was someone else's fault.[4]

The problem is illustrated by news accounts of a young man who was convicted of several burglaries when he was twenty-two years of age, years before he committed a burglary that resulted in a murder charge, that could get him a death sentence. Facing a stiff sentence to a state penitentiary on the earlier burglaries, he told the court he wanted to apologize to his parents, who were in court, and that he wished his victims were present to hear him tell them he was "sorry for the things I did." He continued, "I keep hearing from the prosecutor that I'm a wild animal. I'm not." The judge was neither impressed nor persuaded by this testimony during the sentencing hearing and sentenced him to nine years in prison, including six years on parole.[5] I suspect the reason the judge did not accept his apology was that he and his lawyer almost in the same breath told the court that his crime spree was the result of "personal trouble, including learning disabilities, childhood sexual abuse and the revelation at age fourteen that he had been adopted as a baby."[6]

Apparently he learned from this mistake and convinced the parole board to release him in April 2007 in violation of its rules. But he did not learn anything that made him change his behavior as evidenced by the fact that in less than three months out of prison he had committed another burglary and several murders.[7]

This story is the reason that people in the criminal justice system and the politicians who play on the fears of citizens always err on the side of keeping criminals in prison as long as possible, especially those like this person who started his criminal career so early and failed to accept responsibility for his behavior. It also shows how difficult it is for parole boards to determine which inmates are deserving of a second chance.

Although it is probably not a good idea to talk about the crime that you were prosecuted for, writing poems about how you feel is an effective way to deal with anger, frustration, and psychic pain. In some prison contexts there may be security rules against inmates' writing poems which may contain coded messages. Be sure you know the rules of the prison before you put your thoughts on paper and that you stay within the bounds of the advice of legal counsel. But writing can be an excellent way to release pent-up emotions and stay sane.[8]

Writing short stories about your life can not only be therapeutic, but also can help you get in touch with the "narrative themes" that are "driving factors" in your behavior.[9] As helpful as this process may be, the stories that are told or written in jail or prison should be limited to the context of psychotherapy or other confidential relationship which offers protection from disclosures that may create new legal problems or exacerbate the ones you already have. Being too transparent about the particular crime that got you in trouble should not be done without the advice of counsel even after your release. Getting the help you need often involves talking with counselors about the most intimate details of your life. But until it can be done with reasonable assurance that your confidence will not be breached, you will have to find some other way to deal with your pain.

There are theorists who argue that you can improve your mental health by reading self-help books. This process is called biblio-therapy.[10] It is considered so effective that some mental health professionals are prescribing self-help books for people with mental health problems. Although biblio-therapy is not a substitute for standard treatment options, it has been found to be effective in dealing with less severe symptoms of depression, alcohol abuse, and anxiety disorders. It was less effective in dealing with addiction to smoking and "severe alcohol abuse." The conclusion of researchers is that biblio-therapy is "most effective when used in conjunction with conventional therapy or while waiting for conventional therapy to begin."[11] It may be particularly valuable to you while you are behind bars with limited access to regular psychiatric care. The more insight you develop into your condition, the more likely you will be able to manage it without allowing it to control or diminish your life.

8.3 STRESS MANAGEMENT

Check the Way You Handle Pressure

For some people, pressure or stress is an occasion to use drugs or get drunk. Bad idea! For others, stress is handled in other inappropriate ways that are just as bad. How you handle pressure is a good indication of your prospects outside of prison. Scholars have observed that our tolerance for pain has declined. The same can be said for our ability to handle pressure. This may explain the epidemic of drug addiction and alcoholism and why we can not "just say no." But that is no excuse for bad behavior. It is possible to let off steam responsibly. Some do it through sports. Others use meditation—or religion. It can be done!

No one has a greater stake in successful stress management than an ex-inmate because it may very well determine whether he or she stays out of prison or goes back in.

Learn How to Handle Stress

Everybody has stressors. The difference is in how they are handled. Using drugs and alcohol are the worst possible ways to handle pressure because they lead to even bigger problems. Some people say, "I am too blessed to be stressed," or "too anointed to be disappointed." They are either in denial or do not know what they are talking about. Even devoutly religious people have problems—and enough of them will create stress.

The key to managing stress is recognizing it. In extreme cases, medical attention or mental health treatment may be necessary. But for most of us, the stress may just be a sign that we are over worked, our priorities are wrong, or our relationships need to be improved. Sometimes dealing with stress is as simple as getting rid of the stressors that cause our stress and distress by changing jobs or friends. An old doctor told me that when he was married to a "red head" he had a heart attack by the time he was forty. But when he got rid of her through divorce, he had not had any more trouble, and he was then about eighty. Learning to meditate will also do wonders. But quiet time with God in prayer will do even more to relieve anxiety and stress.

8.4 ANGER

Don't Get Burned by Anger

Anger, a powerful emotional reaction to life's irritants and stressors, is responsible for a lot of negativity. But it does not have to be that way in every instance. There are some things such as injustice that we should be angry about. Anger in that case is normal and healthy if it is handled appropriately. But it should not be used as an excuse to over react to a real or imagined slight. The Bible says be angry but sin not (Ephesians 4:31 NKJV). It means do not let it last too long. As the Bible puts it, "Do not let the sun go down on your wrath." If you are so angry that you lose control of yourself, you need more help than this book will provide. If your anger is producing that effect, you need individual counseling or therapy from a mental health professional. A good book on anger management may help you obtain insight into what "ticks you off."

It is possible that the root of your problem is unhappiness with yourself. That is often the case with people who are unable to forgive themselves. They have locked themselves into an emotional prison and thrown away the key. Freedom from this place of confinement may be as simple as forgiving and accepting yourself, even when you think the problem is with someone else. The philosopher was right who said, "We see things not as they are but as we are."[12]

Another source of anger for many young men is an absent father. The solution is simple as forgiving him and moving on. Anger can be a friend or foe, depending on how you let it affect you and how you use it. Used well or appropriately, it can supply the energy to accomplish great goals. If you do not harness it and apply it to worthwhile goals, it can destroy you and any chance you have to make something of yourself. That cannot be done until you own it and acknowledge it. Sometimes people are angry and do not know it or do not know why. You cannot deal with it until you know where it is coming from. As John Hagee, the popular televangelist says, "You cannot change what you will not confront."

As I have heard one of my friends say often, "Acid does more harm to the vessel in which it is stored than the object on which it is poured." As anger can hurt you and keep you from succeeding if it is not handled appropriately, you should get some help managing it. Learning how to express anger without allowing it to make you physically sick, depressed, or resort to anti-social behavior is the key to managing yourself. This is also good advice for the people who love you. They are often just as angry with you for repeatedly letting them down as you are about your circumstances.

CHAPTER NINE
The Secret of Staying Straight

If there is anything more important than getting oneself straight, it is staying straight. With all of the temptation to do wrong and the easy access to drugs in our communities, regardless of one's socio-economic status, that is easier said than done. But for you, failure is not an option.

For many people, their life has been a series of efforts by other people to straighten them out. But the thesis of this book is that no one can do that but you. This is illustrated by the story that one of my colleagues tells about a minister who left a big church to go to work for a funeral home. When asked why he left a big church to take up his new line of work, he replied, "I got tired of straightening folk out at that church. Every time I would straighten them out they got crooked again. Down here at this funeral home when I straighten a fellow out, he stays straight." That is the only way anyone other than yourself can keep you straight. This chapter offers some concluding advice on how you can keep yourself straight, without ending up in a funeral home or prison.

9.1 GET A LIFE THAT'S WORTH LIVING

Look at Your Life

Too few folk have a real life. Their life is centered on things and pleasure. The result is that they use people in order to get things and meet other needs. In the end, their lives are empty and meaningless because they do not realize that "man does not live by bread alone, but by every word that proceeds from the mouth of God!" Many people have no life. When they are told to "get a life," they do not have a clue as to how to do it.

The key to getting a life is getting a relationship with God! He supplies the principles by which we should live and everything else we need to have a life that is worth living. The poet was right: "The unexamined life is not worth living."

See What Other Folk Think about You

I have heard many people say they do not care what others think about them. That is flat wrong. Other people can see things about you that you can't see. Sometimes we do not realize that we have a problem until people who love us call it to our attention. Getting an honest appraisal of your attitude, image, and appearance from somebody you trust will help you deal with things you cannot see. All of us have blind spots. Caveat: If you value and want honest feedback, do not argue or get mad with the person you asked for feedback. To do you any good, it has to be honest. If it becomes the subject of argument, the person you asked to give you an opinion may either refuse or tell you what you want to hear. If you trust the person enough to ask for feedback, listen and evaluate what was said. Take what you can use and discard the rest. But don't argue or get mad!

Get Your Civil Rights Restored

Informed voting and other forms of responsible civic participation will give you a stake in your community. They will also give you powerful incentives to stay out of trouble—if you need anything else after what you have been through. But more importantly getting your rights restored will transform you from a "dead man" into a person who is alive. When you are convicted, you die civilly and socially. Getting your rights restored is the first step towards affirming that you are now alive and that even "dry bones" can come back to life.

A lot of your fellow Americans do not vote. In that sense they are no better than you because they can vote and will not do it. They are like people who can read but do not do it. It is still true as someone has observed, those who can read and do not are no better than those who cannot read.

In a real sense, it is true that if you do not vote you do not count. It is a step towards making your life count. Besides, it does not make good sense for a former prisoner to say that his prosecution and incarceration were political and not register as soon as possible and vote to hold the people involved in the system accountable for the way they administer the criminal justice system. But the object of civic participation is not revenge, but community improvement. Continuing to say that you are victim of someone else's conduct may be evidence that you are blaming everybody but yourself for your predicament and not accepting personal responsibility for it. What I am challenging you to do is live like a citizen. Citizenship comes with many privileges. But it also entails great obligations, which, at a minimum, involve respect for the rule of law and conformity to reasonable standards of conduct—not just registering to vote. Only after you accept this challenge can you become reconnected to society. Everything I have said so far is aimed at getting you to this point.

Recognize the Difference between Being Golden
and Becoming Someone else's Gold

Some of you would not go to school, work, or learn a skilled trade. Now you are the raw material for the prison industry. The raw material for the prison industry is consistently being replenished. What is needed for it to function is the ultimate renewable resource. In case you have not figured it out yet, you are it. When jails are built, they all fill up. Private prisons are built on the basis of the philosophy that "if you build it they will come"— and do they ever!

The numbers are staggering. About seven million adults, representing almost three percent of the U.S. population, were incarcerated, on probation or on parole at the end of 2005. That included 2.2 million people in federal and state prisons or local jails, 4.1 million on probation and more than 784,000 on parole.[1]

In 2005, 40 percent of those imprisoned were black, 35 percent whites, and 26 percent Hispanics. To make matters worse, there are studies which predict that the number of inmates in U.S. prisons will rise by thirteen percent in the next five years.[2]

Little attention is given to rehabilitation in the face of sky rocketing rates of incarceration. Further, funding for the educational programs and vocational training has not been increased to meet the need. So far there is not enough promise of a high return on capital to induce investors to take on this hard work. Besides, when you start talk about rehabilitation, someone is likely to ask for proof that it works. When you lock people up, the only question that is likely to be asked is whether the prison is secure. It is always easier to justify budget requests based on the number of arrests and convictions than it is to explain the need for crime prevention programs that attempt to rehabilitate prisoners.

In a year's time, as many as 13.5 million people spend time in jails or prisons and 95 percent return to their community of origin. What is worse, they do not return better. They are responsible for additional crimes when they are released and may be contributing to the rise in the incidence of infectious diseases such as HIV, hepatitis or tuberculosis.[3]

This condition caused USA Today to conclude that 95 percent of inmates are freed as trained in violence, short on rehabilitation.[4] To make matters worse, there is a failure to recognize that the violence in prison follows prisoners when they go home and there is "a severe lack of programs to help prisoners prepare for re-entry to society."[5] This undoubtedly contributes to recidivism. But the answer is not in programs but in persons. That is where responsibility for solving this problem rests.

Corporate America is bullish on you because you make businesses possible that provide goods and services to communities that provide alternatives to publicly financed jails and prisons. In the spirit of capitalism, these businesses see an opportunity where others see a problem and as a result they are making huge profits off people like you.

All of this means that corporate America sees prison as a "growth business." According to the *Wall Street Journal*, "Crowded jails, stretched state budgets, mandatory sentencing and a border crackdown have sent the profit shares of the nation's biggest private prison operation, Correction Corporation of America, soaring. This company manages more than 60 state and federal detention facilities in 19 states and Washington, D.C., through a process known as "out-sourced incarceration."[6] The result is that investors are smiling all the way to the bank over your adversity. It also means that they have a powerful incentive to keep you locked up as long as possible.

Your presence in jail or prison creates other business opportunities for business people. For example, there is a demand for professional portable jail cells because of over-crowding and tight budgets. Prison cells are a $600 million market. The need to control prison men and women is that a facility needs maximum security, handcuffs and barbed wire. That is a $1.5 billion dollar market.[7] Instead of a human being, you have been reduced by your behavior to just another business opportunity for someone else to exploit.

For the big business segment of society, you are worth more behind bars than on the streets. The cold reality is that there is little or no profit in trying to reform people who are hell bent on destroying their lives and making everybody else's life miserable in the process. But once you cross the line, and engage in criminal conduct that gets you thrown in prison, your value instantly rises. The people who benefit from the increase in your value are the shareholders of the corporations that supply the cells and security paraphernalia that are necessary to keep you behind bars in private for profit prisons—not you! In this limited sense, crime does pay—but only for corporate shareholders. Make no mistake about it; crime will never pay for you. There is little or no future or benefit in crime for you. Anything you get from it is "fools gold." How does it feel to be valued for your ability to make somebody rich by occupying a jail cell? Is that the best you can do with your life?

The problem of prison overcrowding has become so acute that prisoners have become part of interstate commerce as exports from one state to another. When one states' prisons become inadequate, instead of building new facilities, they are increasingly sending prisoners hundreds of miles across state lines, sometimes to other state prisons but most often to private prisons.[8] This peripatetic prison population is estimated to be ten thousand at this point. In the overall scheme of things, that is a relatively small number, but it is likely to increase. In anticipation of that, the Corrections Corporation of America has made a commitment to spend $213 million on construction and renovation projects for five thousand prisoners by 2008.[9]

The effect of sending inmates from prison to prison interferes with vocational training and rehabilitation programs. It also disrupts inmates' ability to maintain ties to their families. These negative consequences of state prisoners—and out-of-state transfers is that this policy makes it more difficult to keep inmates from committing new crimes after their release. Although there are no studies that specifically examine the effect of out-of-state prisoner transfers, there are studies of recidivism which found that inmates who maintain family contacts through visits and telephone calls are less likely to violate their parole or commit new offenses.[10]

Keep doing what you have been doing and you will continue to help improve the bottom line of corporate jailers. You can change this when you decide you would rather be golden instead of being someone else's gold.

9.2 RELIGION

Don't Forget the Promises You Made
Follow through on the commitment that you made while in jail or prison. Remember how you prayed every day and night for your freedom? Remember the promises

you made God in the presence of many witnesses? Now is the time to act on what you promised. The folk who heard your prayer and promises will not know what became of you or the promises you made. But God will!

You may not be accountable to anyone else, but you are answerable to your maker. The highest and best expression of gratitude is a transformed life. If you are not there yet, get into a worship service every Sunday and a Bible study in the middle of the week. Worship will do more for you than anything else if you go listening for the voice of God and respond with faith to what you hear.

Do Not Be Surprised If Churches Do Not Help You

Howard Thurmond lamented how poor a job ministers have done in explaining the meaning of Christianity "to the man who stands with his back against the wall." In his view, "The masses of men live with their backs constantly against the wall."[11]

We have not done much better in speaking to those who are locked up behind walls. Few churches have prison ministries because they have failed to see that the people behind bars are our sons and daughters who deserve a second chance. Further, they have failed to communicate the message of the gospel to people who read what it says to those who are struggling to survive a prison experience as much as those who are dealing with oppression on the outside.

Deal with Temptation

As Dr. Karl Menninger says, "Crime is every person's temptation."[12] That is true whether he is a "peon or potentate." The problem is not in being tempted. It is yielding to the temptation. But every time you say no to temptation it helps you in future encounters with evil. As the songwriter put it, "Yield not to temptation for yielding is sin—each victory will help you some other to win." In other words, every time you say "no," you are in a better position to say it in future encounters with temptation.

I suspect that temptation is conduct-specific. By that I mean that we are only tempted to commit acts that we have a particular vulnerability or susceptibility to because of personal tastes, habits, or weakness. The devil shrewdly exploits people based on this principle. We are rarely tempted to do something we do not already have a strong predisposition to do. When a person is caught in a law enforcement "sting," the usual defense is "I was entrapped." But that "dog won't hunt" if you were predisposed already and the "sting" only provided the opportunity. For all of these reasons, it is a good idea to avoid things that tempt you to do evil or commit criminal acts.

For example, something as simple as looking at pictures of children has been found to be associated with acts of sexual abuse against minors. The conclusion of this study is that downloading sexual images from the internet of children often results in molestation when the opportunity presents itself. In other words, if you possess child pornography, you are at risk of molesting children.[13] There are many other things that will tempt you. If you want to stay out of jail or prison, it is up to you to know yourself well enough to know what you are vulnerable to and avoid it.

Distinguish Between Asking for Help and Begging

Starting your new life by begging for what you need is not likely to make a good impression. Having said that, it is important to emphasize that you have to crawl before you walk. To facilitate this transition from crawling to walking, most communities have a resource list that contains free survival resources and social services. Typical resources include food, clothes, and shelter. Some provide help with utilities, medical care, and prescriptions. For things you need that cannot be obtained free, you may find them at a reduced price at thrift stores run by the Salvation Army, Goodwill Industries or even private entrepreneurs.

As part of your pre-release planning, you should obtain a community resource list long before you are released. A good place to begin in most communities is the United Way. Their member agencies are committed to helping people in need. Many churches have ministries that will offer some assistance. But in most communities, the best place to go is the Salvation Army or Rescue Mission. They know how to spot con artists. But they also know how to help people like you with a variety of essential services and at the same time insist on accountability.

How much help you receive depends upon you and the nature of your crime. The people you ask for help have a right to know what you have done out of concern for their personal protection. That is as true of church people as it is of any other potential source of help. Just because they are saved does not mean they are suckers. Consequently, be prepared to answer honestly any questions you are asked by people you ask for help. Remember, you asked for help. It may be your business, but you make it others' business by asking them for help.

There is a difference between a hand-out and a hand-up. In presenting yourself as someone who is interested in getting up, you are more likely to get help than if you come across as a beggar who is looking for a hand-out. In the former, what is offered will be seen as help. But in the latter, it will be viewed as facilitation of alcoholism, addiction or sorryness.

I grew up in a single parent home on welfare. When I went off to school, a lot of good people gave me a "helping hand." I was trying to make my life better, and I was willing to work for what I wanted. When people see that you are trying to do right they will help you. But, if they think you are just trying to "get over on them" they will not give you the time of day! Watch the scam used by people who stand at intersections and hold a sign which says "will work for food." While a few people may say "but for the grace of God there go I," most people roll up their windows and ignore them without giving them a dime. The reason is either they think they should work for what they want, if it's nothing more than "flipping burgers," or that they are being conned. Success on the outside of prison requires you to deal with other people's perceptions and expectations.

This is a challenge that you will face for a long time, even though you have paid your debt to society. But do not despair. The experience of many people who have been through what you are going through proves that, in time, it is possible to overcome the stigma of criminality that goes along with a criminal record. That does not just happen. It happens through honest and hard work instead of begging or looking for sympathy and asking for something for nothing. Too many people who are down on their luck because of bad choices seem to believe that somebody owes them something. Everything in life that is worthwhile has a price tag on it. If you get anything of value you will have to pay for it.

The election of Senator Barack Obama as the first African American President has caused many people with poor financial prospects to mistakenly believe he is going to solve all of their problems. Do not be deceived into thinking that what happens in Washington, D. C., the state capital or city hall, is going to be more effective in getting you on your feet than what you do for yourself in your local community. Your destiny is in your hands, despite campaign rhetoric that might have led you to think otherwise. All the President can do is make sure that the playing field is level. After that, you, like everybody else, are on your own!

AFTER WORD

When I was almost a teenager, some of my friends went into a neighborhood within walking distance from where we lived and broke out the windows of one or more abandoned houses. Someone saw them and called the police. They were arrested. The only reason I did not get arrested is that for once I was not with them when this mindless act of vandalism occurred.

I never will forget the verbal abuse my friends endured long after their ordeal was over. They were reviled with the question, "What kind of bird can't fly?" With great glee and laughter came the answer, "A jailbird."

I have thought about that a lot. Someone has well said that angels with broken wings can fly "when they embrace each other." That is the basis of my belief that people in prison or those who have been released are not jailbirds, but angels with broken wings who can fly again when they embrace those who have their interests at heart, their family, and God.

The only thing that kept me from getting into trouble with my friends was the fact that I was not with them when they got into their mischief. But there were plenty of times when I got into "devilment," as my mother called it, by myself and sometimes with my friends. It is only because of the love and discipline of my mother and the grace of God that it did not become a way of life. Every time I left home I got a sermon that said "be back here before dark," "don't put your hands on anything that does not belong to you," and "make something out of yourself." The only difference between me and you and a lot of other people is that I didn't get caught before what my mother said sank in my sometimes "hard head." I remember her asking me more than once, "Boy, what makes your head so hard?" All I could say was, "I don't know ma'am." My point in saying this is that all of us have been where you are and faced the same temptations. What I say is not offered out of a sense of superiority. But I am convinced that the same grace that saved me from a useless life is also available to you. Perhaps that is what Clarence S. Darrow, the famous defense attorney, meant when he said, "I do not believe there is any sort of distinction between the real moral conditions of the people in and out of jail. One is just as good as the other."[1]

What kind of bird are you? A colleague tells a story about an eagle who thought he was a chicken. He had to learn that he was meant to soar through the air instead of hanging out on the ground in a barn yard.

If you have been looking up and never been quite satisfied with where you are, that may be a good indication that you are an eagle instead of a chicken. Unfortunately, it took getting locked up in a cage for you to discover the difference between a chicken and an eagle. Perhaps, that is what Oscar Wilde meant when he wrote:

I never saw a man who looked with such a wistful eye upon that little tent of blue which prisoners call the sky.[2]

If you have to be a jailbird, it is far better to be an eagle than a chicken. At least the eagle has in him the possibility of flight. If prison helps you understand who you are and prepares you for your eventual return to the sky, then it might be the best thing that ever happened to you. There is no telling how high you will go when you "straighten up and fly right." As an aside, Benjamin Franklin thought that a turkey was a better national symbol than an eagle because he considered eagles to be of bad moral character. This judgment was based on their predatory nature which was not unlike the way some people live. This negative judgment was rejected and the eagle, because of its strength and majesty, became this nation's symbol.[3]

There are several examples of ex-jailbirds who managed to fly again. One by the name of Peter flew out of prison by the power of the Holy Spirit. Another one by the name of Nelson Mandela flew so high that he landed in the Presidency of South Africa. Yet another by the name of Martin Luther King, Jr., achieved international acclaim for leading the fight against racial injustice.

Arguably, a jailbird is an eagle who thinks he is a chicken. The task of this book is to help eagles overcome the identity crisis and confusion that have made them earth-bound valley dwellers when they were meant for the sky and mountain peaks.

The sad truth is that no one is immune to trouble. Prisons are full of people of all ages. Some of them got in trouble late in life after escaping the youthful indiscretions that tempt all of us. All of us are at risk. The worst thing that can happen is destroying our lives at the noon hour—or later. Just because we did not get caught in our youth is no guarantee that bad habits will not catch up with us when we get old. The words of Dr. Karl Menninger express my views on this far better than I can say it:

Crime is everybody's temptation. It is easier to look with proud disdain upon "those people who got caught – the stupid ones, the unlucky ones, the blatant ones… Most crimes go undetected, including ours.[4]

Although what Dr. Menninger said is probably true, the fact remains that most people do not become criminals. What Stanton E. Samenow says also rings true. Most people do not become criminals even when they come from bad homes or grow up in poverty.

All of us know people who get away with murder and lesser crimes because of who they are and their status in life. While you can take solace from the fact that they are no better than you, do not attempt to be like them. Eventually people who commit criminal acts get caught—regardless of their smarts, or resources.

When you get out of prison, I sincerely hope it will be for good and that what I have had to say will not only help you continue your rehabilitation, but also help you stay out of trouble. Given the cost of locking up so many of our citizens, it is possible to ask who is the prisoner—you or society? It is arguable that if you leave prison for good, you will in the process set those who bear the heavy cost of your incarceration free.

SUGGESTED FOLLOW-UP READING LIST

Abramsky, Sasha. *American Furies: Crime, Punishment, and Venegence in the Age of Mass Imprisonment*. Boston: Beacon Press, 2007.

Aviely, Don. *Predictably Irrational: The Hidden Forces That Shape Our Decisions*. New York:. Harper, 2008.

Bible (I suggest a modern language verison such as the New King James Version).

Blackmon, Douglas A. *Slavery by Another Name: The Re-Enslavement of Black People In America From Civil War to World War II*. New York: Doubleday, 2008.

Cheever, Joan M. *Back From the Dead: One Woman's Search for the Men Who Walked off America's Death Row*. Chichester, West Sussex, England: John Wiley & Sons Ltd, 2006.

Colson, Charles W. *Born Again*. New York: Benton Books, 1976.

Covey Stephen R. *The 7 Habits of Highly Effective People: Powerful Lessons in Personal Change*. New York: Simon & Schuster, Inc., 1989.

Downie, Leonard Jr. *Justice Denied : The Case for Reform of The Courts*. Baltimore. Penguin Books, Inc., 1971.

Golemen, Daniel. *Emotional Intelligence: Why It Can Matter More Than IQ*. New York: Bartom Books, 2005.

Grossman, Ned. *How To Succeed In Life: Ideas and Principles They Don't Teach In School*. Shaker Heights, Ohio: Diamond Publishing Company, 1994.

Haley, Alex. *The Autobiography of Malcolm X*. New York: Ballantine Publishing Group. 1990.

Hill, Napoleon. *Law of Success. The 21st Century Edition*. Los Angeles: High Roads Media, Inc., 2003.

Hirsh, Andrew Von. *Doing Justice: The Choice of Punishments*. New York: Hill and Wang, 1976.

Hartford, Tim. *The Logic of Life: The Rational Economics of an Irrational World*. New York: Random House, 2008

Kelley, Anthony. *Jailhouse Religion: The Church's Mission and Ministry to the Incarcerated*. Nashville: Townsend Press, 1992.

Lichtenstein, Alex. *Twice the Work of Free Labor: The Political Economy of Convict Labor in the New South*. London: Verso, 1996.

Martin, Joseph C. *Chalk Talks on Alcohol*. San Francisco: Harper San Francisco, 1973.

McCall, Nathan. *Makes Me Want to Holler*. New York: Random House, 1994.

Menninger, Carl. *The Crime of Punishment*. New York: The Viking Press, 1966.

Meranze, Michael. *Laboratories of Virtue: Punishment, Revolution and Authority in Philadelphia, 1760-1835*. Chapel Hill: University of North Carolina Press, 1996.

Peck, M. Scott. *The Road Less Traveled*. New York: Simon & Schuster, 1978.

Petersilia, Joan. *When Prisoners Come Home: Parole and Prisoner Reentry (Studies in Crime and Public Policy)*. Oxford: Oxford University Press, 2003.

Samenow, Stanton E. *Inside the Criminal Mind*. New York: Crown Publishers, 2004.

Spitale, Lennie. *Prison Ministry: Understanding Prison Culture Inside and Out*. Nashville: Broadman & Holman Publishers, 2002.

Spitale, Lennie. *The State of Black America: Portrait of the Black Male*. New York: National Urban League, 2007.

Travis, Jeremy. *But They All Come Back: Facing the Challenges of Prisoner Reentry*. Washington, D.C.: The Urban Institute Press, 2005.

Vollen, Lola and Dave Eggers. *Surviving Justice: America's Wrongfully Convicted*. San Francisco: McSweeney's Books, 2005.

Warren, Rick. *The Purpose Driven Life*. Grand Rapids, Michigan: Zondervan, 2002.

Zimbardo, Phillip. *The Lucifer Effect: Understanding How Good People Turn Evil*. New York: Random House, 2007.

INDEX

END NOTES

INTRODUCTION
1   J. Donald Evans, ed., *Poems of Ralph Waldo Emerson*. (New York: Thomas Y. Crowell Company, 1965), p. 106.
2   Richard Newman, ed. *African American Quotations*. New York: Checkmark Books, 2000), p. 258.
3   George Will, "Lower Crime Rate A thorn for Liberals." *Atlanta Journal-Constitution*, June 22, 2008, p. 3.
4   Ibid.
5   Ibid.
6   Richard Newman, ed. *African American Quotations*. (New York: Checkmark Books, c2000), p. 258.
7   Harold J. Clinebell, Jr. *Basic Types of Pastoral Counseling*. (Nashville: Abingden Press, 1966), p. 39-40.
8   Fred R. Shapiro, ed. *The Yale Book of Quotations*. (New Haven: Yale University Press, 2006), p. 210.
9   Solomon Moore, "Justice Department Numbers Show Prison Trends," *The New York Times*, December 6, 2007, p. A-16.
10 Elisabeth Kubler-Ross, *On Death and Dying*. New York: The McMillan Company, 1969), p. 38f.
11 Fernanda Santos and Janet Roberts, "Putting a Price on a Wrongful Conviction." *The New York Times*. Sunday Week, December 12, 2007, p. 4.
12 "At 60% of Total, Texas is Breaking Execution Trends: U. S. Dispositions Growing. State carries out 26 of 42 Death Sentences Nationwide." *The New York Times*, December 26, 2007, p. A-1.
13 P. Edward Ernest, ed., *The Family Album of Favorite Poems*. (New York: Grossett & Dunlap, 1959), p.180.

CHAPTER ONE
1   Andrew Von Hirsh, *Doing Justice: The Choice of Punishment*. (New York: Hill and Wang, c1976), p.11.
2   Joan Petersilia, *When Prisoners Come Home: Parole and Prisoner Reentry*. (Oxford: Oxford University Press, 2003), p. 65.
3   Ibid.
4   *The State of Black America 2007: Portrait of the Black Male*. (New York: National Urban League, 2007), p. 75f.
5   Petersilia, op.cit, p. 53.
6   Ibid, p. 13.
7   Ibid, p. 112, 116, 124-126.
8   Idid, p. 120-123.
9   Ibid, p. 112-116.
10 Ibid, p. 41-42.
11 Ibid.
12 Ibid.
13 Ibid.
14 Ibid, p. 121.
15 Ibid, p. 40-41.
16 Bryan A. Garner, ed., *Black's Law Dictionary*. (7th edition, St. Paul: West Law Group, 1999), p. 1290.

17   Ibid, p. 1276.

18   Von Hirsch, op.cit. p. 11f.

19   Ibid.

20   Karl Menninger, *The Crime of Punishment*. (New York: The Viking Press, 1968), p. 81f.

21   Ibid.

22   Ibid.

23   Sam Roberts, "Violent felons move forward with law suit over parole," *The New York Times*, December 30, 2007, p.A20.

24   Paul Lawrence Dunbar, *The Complete Poems of Paul Lawrence Dunbar* (New York: Dodd, Mead, and Company, 1913), p.22.

25   George Will, "Lower Crime Rate A Thorn for Liberals," *Atlanta Journal-Constitution*, June 22, 2008, p. c-3. See also Steven D. Levitt and Stephen J. Dubner, *Freakonomics: A Rogue Economist Explores the Hidden Side of Everything*. (New York: William Morrow, 2005), p. 22f.

26   Ibid.

27   Cynthia Tucker, "Just Filling Prisons Won't Make Us Safer," *Atlanta Journal-Constitution*, June 29, 2008, p. c-6.

28   Washington, D.C., The Urban Institute Press, 2005. For additional resources on reentry programs see the website of the prison where you or a member of your family are incarcerated. Many of them feature reentry resource lists on college education, housing, and other services. See, for example, www.dcor.state.ga.us.
      Also, see Amy L. Soloman et al, *Life after Lockup: Improving Reentry from Jail to the Community*. Washington, D.C. Urban Institute, 2008). This publication offers reentry resources for people who are in jail or on probation. It also suggests that although there are many challenges associated with jails, they also offer opportunitites to provide early intervention in local communities that may reduce the number of people in jail who eventually go to prision even for thode who receive short sentences. An additional resource is Jeff Mellow, et a, *The Jail Administraor's Tool Kit for Reentry*. (Washiington, D. C.: The Urban Institute, 2008).

29   Richard Newman, ed., *African American Quotations*. (New York: Checkmark Books, 2000), p. 258.

30   Fred R. Shapiro, *The Yale Book of Quotations*. (New Haven: Yale University Press, 2006), p. 656.

31   2007 U. S. Lexis, 13083 (2007).

32   Ibid., p. 2-3.

33   Ibid., p. 4.

34   Ibid., p. 10

35   Ibid., p. 2.

36   Michael S. Schmidt, "While Government Makes Case, Dogs Remain in Confinement," *The New York Times*. August 1, 2007, p. c-12.

37   Schmidt, op.cit. See also, e.g. Mary Ann Mott, "Michael Vick Fighting Dogs Get 'Rehab' Care," *National Geographic News*, January 28, 2008, *National Geographic News*.com/News; Bridgid Schulte, *Saving Michael Vick's Dogs*. Washington Post.com, July 7, 2008; Juliet MaCur, "Given Reprieve N.F.L. Star's Dogs find Kindness." *New York Times*, NYTimes.com, February 2, 2008.

38   Ibid.

39   George Sweeting, ed., *Great Quotes and Illustrations*. (Waco, Texas: Word Books, 1985), p. 69.

CHAPTER TWO

1   This idea has been expressed by many thinkers. William James, e.g., said something similar. See, e.g., Ned Grossman, *How to Succeed in Life*. (Shaker Height, Ohio, 1999: viewed public copy) p. 74f, 82.

2   Tom Butler-Bowdon, ed., *50 Spiritual Classics: Timeless Wisdom from 50 Great Books of Inner Discovery, Enlightenment and Purpose*, (New York: MJF Books, 2005), p. 2-3

3   Ibid., p.133

4   Ibid.

5   Ibid., p. 135

6   *Think and Grow Rich*. (New York: Farcett Crest, 1960), p. 175.

7   Ibid, p. 176

8   Ibid.

9   Ibid., p. 190-191

10   Ibid.

11   Ibid.

12   Butler-Bowden, op.cit., p. 133-134.
13   See O.C.G.A. § 17-10-6.1 (Georgia Crimal Code)
14   Ibid.
15   Joan Petersilia, *When Prisoners come Home: Parole & Prisoner Reentry.* (Oxford: Oxford University Press, 2003), p. 22-23.
16   These words are from a sermon by Dr. A. Louis Patterson at the Congress of Christian Education of the National Baptist Convention, U.S.A, Inc. circa 2004.
17   P. Edward Ernest, ed., *The Family Album of Favorite Poems.* (New York: Grossett & Dunlap, 1959), p. 25.
18   Robert Young, *Young's Analytical Concordance.* (Grand Rapids: Associated Publishers,), p. 916.
19   (Grand Rapids, Michigan: Zondervon, 2002).
20   Rick Hampson, "Anti-snitch Campaign Riles Police, Prosecutors," *USA Today*, March 29, 2006, p.1-A, 2-A.
21   Ibid
22   Robert Axelrod, *The Evolution of Cooperation.* (Cambridge: Basic books, 1980), p. 7f. See also, Martin Nowak, "In Games, an Insight into the Rules of Evolution," *New York Times*, July 31, 2007, p. D-1
23   Attributed to Arnold and Clifford Lazarus.
24   *The 7 Habits of Highly Effective People*, (New York: Simon & Schulster, 1989).
25   Grossman, op. cit., p. 113
26   Roy B. Zuck, *The Speaker's Quote Book.* (Grand Rapids: Kregel Publications, 1997), p.166.
27   Grossman, op. cit., p. 108.
28   Ibid.
29   Steven Barboza, ed., *The African American Book of Values: Classic Moral Stories.* (New York: Doubleday, 1998), p.488.

CHAPTER THREE
1   Charles Duhig, "Warning: Habits May Be Good for You." *New York Times*, Sunday, July 13, 2008, p.1.
2   Roy B. Zuck, *The Speaker's Quote Book.* (Grand Rapids, Michigan: Kregel Publications, 1997), p. 184.
3   John Bartlett, *Bartlett's Familiar Quotations.* (Boston: Little, Brown and Company, 1980), p. 384.
4   Lizette Alvarnex, "Army Giving Moral Waivers in Recruiting." *The New York Times*, February 14, 2007, p. A1.
5   Latitia C. Baldor, "Sexual Assault Jump in 2006, Pentagon Says," *Atlanta Journal Constitution*, p. A5, March 27, 2007.
6   Alex Haley, *Autobiography of Malcolm X.* (New York: Ballantine Publishing Company, 1990).
7   This statement is attributed to Lester Maddox, the former segregationist governor of the State of Georgia.
8   William Bennett, *The Book of Virtues: A Treasury of Great Moral Stories.* (New York: Simon & Schuster, 1993).
9   Steven Barboza, *The African American Book of Values: Classic Moral Stories.* (New York: Doubleday, 1998).
10   Suzy Platt, *Respectfully Quoted.* (New York: Barnes & Nobles, Inc., 1993), p.40.

CHAPTER FOUR
1   *The Inferno of Dante.* Robert Pinsky, trans. (New York: Farrar, Straus and Giroux, 1994).
2   Victor Frankl, *Man's Search for Meaning.* (New York: Washington Square Press, 1959), p. 126f.
3   Ibid.
4   Roy b. Zurk, *The Speaker's Quote Book.* (Grand Rapids: Kregel Publications, 1997), p.200.
5   Ibid., p.198.
6   Frankl, op.cit.
7   Zuck, op.cit., p. 275. Also, see Spencer Johnson, *Who Moved My Cheese?* (New York: G.P. Putnan's & Sons, 1998).
8   Steven Barboza. *The African American Book of Values.* (New York: Doubleday 1998), p. 284f.
9   Ned Grossman, *How to Succeed in Life.* (shaker Heights, Ohio: Diamond Publishing Company, 1999), p. 82.
10   Ibid., p. 74.

11 These words are attributed to Frederick Longbridge.

12 Grossman, op.cit., p.80.

13 These words are attributed to Lou Holtz, highly successful football coach and sports commentator.

14 Fred R. Shapiro, *The Yale Book of Quotations*. (New Haven: Yale University Press, 2006), p. 221.

15 Grossman, op.cit., p. 54.

16 Ibid., p.139

17 Allen Loy McGinnis, *Bringing Out the Best in People*. (Minneapolis: Augsbury Publishing House, 1985), p. 31f.

18 Zuck, op.cit., p. 162.

19 Paul Lawrence Dunbar, *The Complete Poems of Paul Lawrence Dunbar*. (New York: Dodd, Mead & Company, 1913), p.8.

20 Zuck, op.cit., p. 185.

21 Authorship of The Serenity Prayer is unsettled. Reinhold Neibuhr, the protestant theologian, is credited by some scholars as its author.

22 These words were written by Langston Hughes, one of the leading poets of the Harlem Rennassance. See Fred R. Shapiro, ed., *The Yale Book of Quotations*. (New Haven: Yale University Press, 2006), p. 375

23 Don Ariely, *Predictably Irrational: The Hidden Forces That Shape Our Decisions*. (New York: Harper, 2008), p. 139f.

24 Ibid.

25 Natasha Singer, "Erasing Tattoes Out of Regret or Simply to Get a Fresh Canvas," *The New York Times*, June 17,2007, p. A-1.

26 College fund.

27 Eric Fromm, *Escape from Freedom*. (New York: Holt, Rinehart, and Winston, 1941).

28 Daniel B. Baker, ed. *Power Quotes*. (New York: Barnes & Noble Books, 1992), p. 106.

29 Ibid., p.22.

30 Richard Newman, ed., *African American Quotations*. (New York: Checkmark Books, 2000), p. 258.

31 The authorship of "The Serenity Prayer" is in dispute. It is usually attributed to Reinhold Niebuhr.

32 Charles Colson, *Born Again*. (New York: Benton Books, 1976), front matter.

33 Pogo was the creation of Walt Kelly, an American Cartoonist, Shapiro, op.cit. p. 418.

34 John Bartlett, *Bartlett's Familiar Quotations*, Emily Morian Beck, ed. (Boston: Little, Brown and Company, 1980), p. 503.

35 John Maxwell, Attitude 101; *What Each Leader Needs to Know*. (Nashville: Thomas Nelson Publishers, 2003), p. 21

36 This statement is often attributed to George Allen, the former coach of the Washington Red Skins of the National Football League, as the explanation of his practice of trading draft picks for veterans which could help him win sooner rather than later.

37 Peter F. Drucker, "Managing Oneself," Harvard Business Review on *Managing Yourself*. (Boston: Harvard Business School Publishing Corp., 2005), p. 151 F.

CHAPTER FIVE

1   *The Master Key to Riches*. (New York: Faucett Crest, 1965), p. 59f.

2   Ralph Waldo Emerson, "On Compensation" in *The Best of Ralph Waldo Emerson*. (Roslyn, N.Y.: Walter J. Black, Inc., 1941), p.147f.

3   Attributed to Gore Vidal.

4   The problems of children of absent fathers are so well known by ordinary people and social scientists that no documentation is necessary.

5   Tim Hartford, *The Logic of Life: The Rational Economics of An Irrational World*. (New York: Random House, 2008), p. 133.

6   Ibid.

7   Ibid.

8   Ibid., p.8.

9   Ibid., p. 4.

10 Ibid.

11 Attributed to Henry Van Dyke.

12 Fred R. Shapiro, ed., *The Yale Book of Quotations*. (New Haven: Yale University Press, 2006), p. 382.

13 Attributed to Corrie Tenboom

14 Walter Bruggeman, *Peace*. (St. Louis: Chalice Press, 2001), p. 41f.

15 Ibid.

16 John Hagee, televangelist and Pastor, made this statement in one of his televised sermons, circa 2007.

17 "The Serenity Prayer" is open to questions. It is frequently attributed to Reinhold Niebuhr.

18 For a small treatise on this subject see, Harry G. Frankfurt, *On Bullshit*. (Princeton: Princeton University Press, 2005).

19 Ned Grossman, *How to Succeed in Life*. (Shaker Heights, Ohio: Diamond Publishing Company, 1999), p.80/

20 Michael E. McLaughlin, Herman and McLaughlin, *Admissibility of Evidence*, 3rd ed. (Norcross, Georgia, Harrison Company Publishers, 1989), p. 197-198.

21 Paul B. Brown, "How Great Leaders Juggle Ideas," *The New York Times*, , p. B-4, June 16, 2007.

22 Daniel Goleman, *Emotional Intelligence: Why It Can Matter More Than IQ*. (New York: Bantom Books, 2005), p.81.

23 Ibid., p. 81f.

24 Ibid.

25 Ibid.

26 Fred R. Shapiro, ed., *The Yale Book of Quotations*. (New Haven: Yale University Press, 2006), p.44.

27 Ibid., p. 612.

28 see, for example, Proverbs 14:15 (Holy Bible).

29 Shapiro, op. cit., p. 612.

30 Christine Wenderoth, "Lying" in *Dictionary of Pastoral Care and Counselling*. Rodney J. Hunter, ed. (Nashville: Abingdon Press, 1990), p. 672.

31 Attributed to Walter Scott, Shapiro, op. cit., p. 675.

CHAPTER SIX

1 A variation of this thought was attributed to Maréchal Villars who said "Defend me from my friends; I can defend myself from my enemies;" John Bartlett, Emily Morison Beck, *Bartlett's Familiar Quotations*. (Boston: Little, Brown and Company, 1980), p. 422, Note 2; Voltaire supposedly said "May God defend me from my friends, I can defend myself from my enemies;" Even Esar, *20,000 Quips and Quotes*. (New York: Barnes & Nobles Books, 1968), p. 330.

2 Howard Thurmond, *Jesus And The Disinherited*. (Nashville: Abingdon Press, 1949), p. 28.

3 P. Edward Ernest, ed., *The Family Album of Favorite Poems*. (New York: Grossett & Dunlap, 1959), p. 180.

4 There are many sources on the issue of restorative justice, such as the internet and scholarly monographs. See, e.g., Joan Petersilia, *When Prisoners Come Home: Parole and Prisoner Reentry*. (Oxford: Oxford University Press, 2003), p. 169f.

CHAPTER SEVEN

1 Bakari Kitwana, *The Hip Hop Generation*. (New York: Basic Civitas Books, 2002), p. 6f.

2 See, for example, the words of B. T. Washington's Atlanta address which, by modern standards is politically unacceptable because of his accomodationist opinions on race relations; E. L. Thornbrough, ed., Booker T. Washington. (Englewood Cliffs, N. J.: Prentice-Hall, Inc., 1969), p. 33f.

3 Roy B. Zuck, *The Speaker's Quote Book*. (Grand Rapids: Kregel Publishing, 1997), p. 276.

4 Gordon E. Jackson, *Labor and Employment Law Desk Book*, Second Edition. (Englewood Cliffs, N. J.: Prentice Hall, Inc., 1993) p. 255.

5 Ibid., p. 254.

6 Ibid., p. 254-255.

7 Ibid.

8 Ibid., p. 254.

9 Ibid.

10 Paul Van Zielberger, "Race A Factor in Job Offers for Ex-Convicts," *The New York Times*, p. A19, June 17, 2005, p. A-19.

11 Ibid.

12 Martin Luther King, Jr., "Facing The Challenge of A New Age," in *Essential Writing and Speeches of Martin Luther King, Jr.*, James Washington, ed. (San Francisco: Harper San Francisco, 1986), p. 139.

13 Ibid.

14   Napoleon Hill, *Think and Grow Rich.* (New York: Fawcett Crest, 1960), p.76.

15   The late Dr. Olen Moyd by his life's work as an imminent scholar and pastor, showed that this is possible. After getting his G.E.D., he earned a bachelors, masters, and Phd degree.

16   Sally Beatty. "Colleges Go Back Behind Bars," *Wall Street Journal,* June 22, 2007, p. W2.

17   Ibid.

18   Kelefa Sanneh, "A Rapper's Prison Time As A Resume Booster," *The New York Times.* The Arts Section, March 24, 2005, p.

19   Jonathan D. Glater, "Crime and Punishment, The Celebrity Version," *The New York Times,* March 6, 2005.

CHAPTER EIGHT

1   One authority says that the percentage of people in prison with drug and alcohol problems is 13 percent of the prison population. See, e.g., Joan Petersilia, *When Prisoners Come Home: Parole and Prisoner Reentry.* (Oxford: Oxford University Press, 2003), p.36f. There are others who claimed that as many as 60 percent have this problem.

2   M. Scott Peck, *The Road Less Traveled.* (New York: Simon and Schuster, 1978. p. 69f.

3   Petersilia, op.cit., p. 36f.

4   Peck, op.cit., p. 35.

5   Allison Leigh Cowan, "Court Papers Sought to Tell Suspect's Story. *The New York Times.* July 31, 2007, p. A-19.

6   Ibid.

7   Ibid.

8   Yoch: J. Dreazen, " The Prison Poets of Guantanamo Find a Publisher," *Wall Street Journal,* June 20, 2007, p. ____.

9   Benedict Carey, "This Is Your Life (And How You Tell It): In story-telling, Deep Clues to the Self," *The New York Times,* May 22, 2007, p. D-1.

10   Helliker, Kevin. "Bibliotherapy: Reading Your Way to Mental Health," *The Wall Street Journal,* July 31, 2007, p. D-1.

11   Ibid.

12   The authorship of these words is questioned. They have been attributed to, among others, Frederick Longbridge.

CHAPTER NINE

1   Mima Mohammed, "Prisons Filled; Most of Drug Crimes," *Atlanta Journal Constitution,* December 1, 2006, p. A-12.

2   Kevin Johnson, "Study Predicts Rise in Inmate Populations," USA Today, February 14, 2007, p. 4A.

3   Ibid.

4   Ibid.

5   "Rising Prison Problems begin to trickle into society," *USA Today,* June 12, 2006, p. 12A.

6   Ian McDonald, "Correction Corporation, finds success in ...," *Wall Street Journal,* May 25, 2007, p. c-1. See also, Stephanie Chen, "Larger Inmate Population is Boon to Private Prisons," *The Wall Street Journal,* November 19, 2008, p. A4.

7   McDonald, op.cit.

8   Ibid.

9   Ibid.

10   Ibid.

11   *Jesus and the Disinherited.* (Nashville: Abingdon Press, 1949), p. 13.

12   Karl Menninger, *The Crime of Punishment.* (New York: The Viking Press, 1968), p. 81f.

13   Julian Sher and Benedict Carey, "Debate on Child Pronography's Link to Molesting," New York Times, July 19, 2007, p. A-1.

AFTER WORD

1   Fred R. Shapiro, ed., *The Yale Book of Quotations.* (New Haven: Yale University Press, p. 185.

2   Ibid., p. 822.

3   Ibid., p. 288. Benjamin Franklin thought that the turkey was a better representative of this nation than the bald eagle.

4   Karl Menninger, *The Crime of Punishment.* (New York: The Viking Press, 1968), p. 81f.